Aztec ornament of turquoise on a wooden base. Gods like
Quetzalcoatl were often conceived in this serpent form.

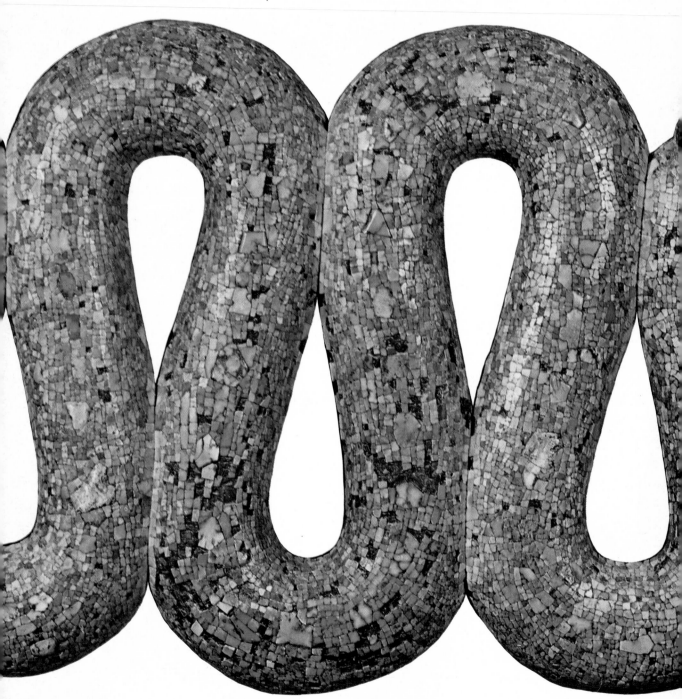

THE ANCIENT WORLD

AN ALDUS BOOK

CURTIS BOOKS
A division of
The Curtis Publishing Company
Philadelphia • New York

A penny bearing the head
of Alfred, the greatest
of the Anglo-Saxon kings.

© Aldus Books Limited, London 1968.
First printing. All rights reserved,
including without limitation
the right to reproduce this book
or portions thereof in any form.
Printed in Germany by Mohndruck, Gütersloh.
Library of Congress Catalog No. 68-26186.

CONTENTS

This is the first of three books surveying world history from the earliest times to the present day. It deals broadly with the dawning civilizations, and with the rise and fall of ancient peoples, city states, kingdoms and empires. It shows in new perspective their inter-relationships, their places in the march of man, and their contributions to the modern world. In such a survey it is not always practical to break off the narrative at the generally accepted limit of ancient times. So this limit has sometimes been ignored, and the theme pursued to its natural conclusion, even though this occurs in the Middle Ages or even later.

EARLY CIVILIZATIONS

Man's progress from a primitive nomad life to a civilized society made a significant advance about 10,000 years ago, when people in the Near East began to grow food crops and rear domesticated animals. By 3000 B.C. people in the Near and Middle East were living in city-states. Already there had been great discoveries and inventions—the wheel, the use of metals, the making of pottery, how to write and count. Craftmanship encouraged trade; and trade, the growth of cities.

Akkad and Sumer

More than 5,000 years ago, a black-haired people called Sumerians began to develop an organized civilization. From the creation of a system of canals for the irrigation of their fields along the Tigris and Euphrates rivers, they went on to build cities, to carry on foreign trade, and to invent a form of writing. By 3000 B.C. Sumerian villages in southern Mesopotamia had already become such major cities as Kish, Lagash and Ur.

Intelligent farmers, builders and inventors, the Sumerians were also hardy warriors. Each city was an independent city – state with a governor known as the *ensi*. In the many conflicts between these city-states, an *ensi* sometimes gained control over another city and became a *lugal*, or king.

In the 24th century B.C. the *ensi* of Umma, Lugal-zaggisi, directed his energies to the conquest and unification of all of Sumer, only to be conquered in turn by another energetic leader, Sargon (about 2306–2250 B.C.), the ruler of the Semitic-speaking people living in Akkad, Sumer's northern neighbor.

Sargon led the defeated Lugal-zaggisi to Kish on a leash, and went on to subdue the rest of Sumer. He also campaigned successfully in northern Syria, Assyria and Elam. His reign lasted 55 years, and his sons and grandson succeeded him. His grandson Naram-Sin (about 2236–2189 B.C.) was the last important king of the Akkadian dynasty. Trade grew in this expanded state, and merchant ships carried goods all along the Persian Gulf.

These Akkadian kings had to contend not only with revolts of the Sumerian cities but also with frequent clashes along the highland borders. One of the mountain peoples to the northeast, the Guti, were at last able to invade the land. They ruled Mesopotamia for almost a hundred years before being overthrown. About 2079 B.C., the Third Dynasty of Ur was founded under Ur-Nammu.

Bronze head of King Sargon of Akkad found at Nineveh dates from about 2306 B.C. This powerful Semitic ruler first conquered Sumer and then extended his kingdom west to the Mediterranean and east to Persia. Two thousand years before the time of Sargon the site of Nineveh on the east bank of the Tigris River (near modern Mosul, Iraq) was occupied. The city was most prosperous in the eighth and seventh centuries B.C. but was destroyed in 612 B.C. by a combined force of Babylonians and Medes.

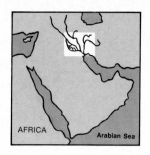

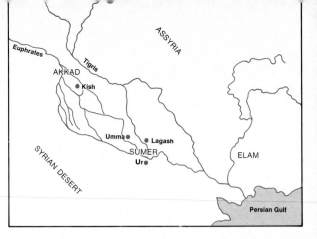

Right: some of the early cities and city-states of Sumer and Akkad in Mesopotamia (between the Tigris and Euphrates Rivers). By 3000 B.C. Sumerian villages had become large cities. At the same time in the north, Akkad's culture and government were Sumerian although the population was Semitic.
Left: map shows position of Sumer and Akkad in relation to other land masses.

During the Third Dynasty of Ur, Sumerian culture, which had not lost its identity under either the Semitic Akkadians or the savage Guti, flourished once more. Religion had always been important in Sumerian life (an *ensi* had for centuries been chief priest as well as ruler, for example), and now more elaborate temples were built to honor the gods.

Called *ziggurats*, or "high places," Sumerian temples were lofty stepped towers rising up to the sky like small mountains. On the top was a shrine to such gods as Anu, the god of heaven, Enki, a water god, and Nannar, a moon god. It has been suggested that the resemblance of ziggurats to mountains recalled some long-ago time when the Sumerians had lived in the highlands and worshipped their gods on mountain peaks.

Because stone and timber had to be imported, Sumerian builders became very skillful in the use of sun-baked bricks made from river mud and crushed reeds. They were probably the first people to learn to use bricks not only for walls but to span the space overhead in arches—probably the first in history—and corbeled vaults.

The royal burial vaults at Ur, which predate the First Dynasty (about 2550 B.C.), contain numerous objects which demonstrate the skill of Sumerian craftsmen. Among these are vessels and ornaments of gold, silver, and copper, cups and bowls of ob-

sidian and lapis lazuli, and wall decorations inlaid with shells, mother-of-pearl, and lapis lazuli. The bones of soldiers and of attendants found in the actual tomb chamber of a king suggest that in these early days a royal burial was also accompanied by human sacrifice.

Excavation has also discovered four-wheeled vehicles dating as far back as 3500 B.C., engraved cylindrical seals used as individual stamps and, most useful for students of this ancient civilization, tablets inscribed with Sumerian ideographic script. From these tablets, archaeologists have deciphered incantations used by priests, chronicles of historical events, business accounts and judicial records.

In their system of mathematics, the Sumerians used the number 60 as the basic unit, from which we have retained the 60-minute hour and the 360-degree circle. The Sumerian calendar marked the times for religious festivals and told the farmers when to plant barley, spelt, onions, and other crops. In order to predict the future, the Sumerians began to observe the heavens as well as reading the entrails of sacrificial animals.

Sumer was finally overrun by Amorites, nomadic tribes of the Syrian Desert, and by Elamites from the east. The city of Ur fell in 1970 B.C., and with the later fall of the dynasties of Isin and Larsa, the story of Babylonia begins.

Relief carved about 2900 B.C. shows warriors from Lagash with tall shields and copper-tipped spears. Constant wars between rival Sumerian cities resulted in the formation of the world's first trained armies. But 700 years later Sumerian forces were defeated by Sargon of Akkad.

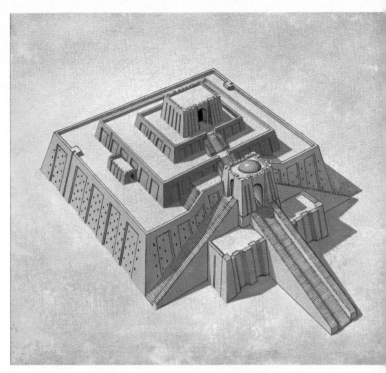

Right: reconstruction of the terraced ziggurat at Ur as it looked about 2000 B.C. Made of millions of bricks, this temple shrine measured about 200 by 150 feet and was 70 feet high (as high as a six-storey building). Stairs at the outside led to the shrine, dedicated to one of the Sumerian gods. This ziggurat was built by the kings of the third dynasty of Ur.

Above: pink limestone, lapis lazuli and shell mosaic showing scenes of Sumerian life about 2600 B.C. Top strip depicts a royal feast; lower two show farmers with animals.

Below: stages in the development of Middle Eastern script from the picture symbols, on the left, of about 3500 B.C., to the cuneiform or wedge-shaped writing of Assyria about 700 B.C.

Above: Sumerians, who probably invented a system of writing before 3000 B.C., wrote with a sharp reed stylus like this on soft clay tablets. These were then baked hard in the sun.

Original pictograph	Later pictograph	Early Babylonian	Assyrian	Original or derived meaning
				bird
				fish
				ox
				grain
				to stand to go

The Valley of the Indus

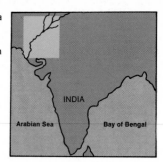

Extending from the Arabian Sea northeast along the Indus River and its tributaries are the towns and cities (shown as dots) that flourished in 2000 B.C. At the height of its power the highly developed Indus civilization probably stretched as far as the Tapti River in Northern India. Right: map shows location of the Indus civilization in India and West Pakistan.

In the 19th century, railroad construction engineers in northwestern India (now Pakistan) unearthed the remains of an ancient city. Located near the former course of the Ravi, a tributary of the great Indus River, the ruins proved to be those of Harappa, built some 4,500 years ago.

Excavations at Harappa and at the city of Mohenjo-Daro, 400 miles southwest along the Indus, have revealed the relics of a highly developed ancient civilization. Since the 1920s more than 40 lesser sites have been discovered.

Of the political history of this civilization there is no record. Although seals have been found inscribed in a pictographic script, no one has yet been able to decipher it. We have only the physical remains of cities and towns from which to reconstruct the life of the Indus Valley people—the first men and women to create a civilization in the great Indian subcontinent.

From the orderly arrangement of the streets of these communities and their elaborate drainage systems we know that there must have been a strong political organization to make the plans and oversee construction. An artificial mound at Mohenjo-Daro seems to have been a citadel, and on its summit are the most impressive buildings of the city: the granary, the Great Bath, two pillared halls, and a building that was probably the residence of some high official, perhaps the chief priest. No buildings have yet been definitely identified as temples nor has any royal tomb been found, though an ordinary grave-yard has been unearthed at Harappa. In a region of river valleys, men made up for lack of building stone by making bricks out of soft river mud, then baking them. Indus builders, using kiln-dried bricks of standard size as a facing over mud bricks, produced brickwork superior to that of the Sumerians (p. 8), their contemporaries who enjoyed the fruits of a civilization even older than their own.

Although what is left of Indus architecture is unpretentious, other crafts show a refined artistic skill. Indus seals, usually small squares of steatite (soapstone), are beautifully carved with animals. There are few examples of stone and bronze sculpture but many small terracottas, which may have been toys or religious objects. The bull, the ox and the water buffalo were popular subjects. Indus pottery was usually made on a wheel and decorated in black. Craftsmen fashioned jewelry of gold, faience, and lapis lazuli; bowls, arrowheads, axes, and other implements and utensils were made of copper and bronze.

This region today is dry with little vegetation, but in the Third millenium B.C. the annual rainfall was two or three times what it is now. The use of kilns for firing bricks indicates that there was an abundance of wood for fuel.

Indus Valley farmers were the first known to have grown cotton, which they spun and wove into cloth and dyed with bright colors. Other crops were barley, wheat, field peas, and probably dates. Bulls, oxen, buffaloes, camels, donkeys, and even ele-

Seal imprints with picture symbols and engravings of a humped bull, a tiger, an elephant and, probably, a god.

phants probably served as beasts of burden. Pigs, cattle, goats and sheep provided meat, milk and wool.

Because the fertility of the valley made a surplus of food possible, a merchant class and a class of skilled craftsmen were able to develop as in Sumer. Indus Valley merchants imported stones and metals from neighboring Rajputana, Baluchistan, and Afghanistan, and some items from lands farther away. Caravans must have traveled far overland, and boats plied along the rivers and the coast. At its height, the Indus civilization extended hundreds of miles along the shore of the Arabian Sea on either side of the mouth of the Indus. It may well be that trade extended up into the Persian Gulf and that there was contact between the people of the Indus Valley and those of Mesopotamia, if not directly, perhaps through some middle station. In any case, organized trade links had been established between the two before and after 2000 B.C. for example, the steatite seals of Indus merchants have been found in Sumer.

The Indus Valley prospered for many centuries, but a gradual deterioration evidently took place, caused by constant floods, overgrazing of the land, continual consumption of trees for firing bricks, and salination of coastal areas. It is possible that the final blow came from an invasion by Aryan peoples from the northwest. By 1200 B.C., the great culture of the Indus Valley people had disappeared.

The Great Bath at Mohenjo-Daro, its floor measuring 39 by 23 feet. The uniform size of the bricks suggests that powerful rulers controlled city building. The city had a grid-iron plan and main streets were 30–45 feet wide. Narrow lanes separated blocks of houses which were several storeys high. Mohenjo-Daro also had a highly developed drainage system.

Relics found in the Indus Valley. Left: bronze statuette of a dancing girl from Mohenjo-Daro. Right: stone bust of a bearded priest-king or god. Working in imported gold and silver, amethyst and lapis lazuli, Indus Valley craftsmen also produced fine bangles, beads and necklaces.

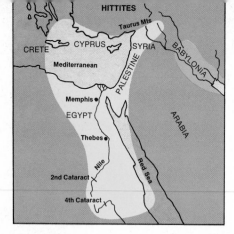

Egypt in Ancient Times

Map shows extent of Egyptian influence in the 15th century B.C. when the power of Egypt was at its height. The sphere of influence included the isles of Crete and Cyprus and stretched into Asia. Egypt's most powerful enemies were the Hittites and Philistines.

In Egypt, as in Mesopotamia and the Indus Valley, the source of a civilization was a river that made the land fertile and provided a natural waterway for trade. The ancient Egyptians, a Hamitic people, called their elongated country the "black land." They began farming the rich black soil along the Nile River about 4500 B.C.

By the fourth millennium there were two kingdoms: Lower Egypt (the Delta area where the Nile emptied into the Mediterranean) and Upper Egypt (the narrow 550 mile-long valley of the Nile south to the first cataract). The unification of the two by Menes and other rulers about 3200 B.C. made Egypt the first true nation in the world.

Menes had been the southern ruler. Now he built a new city, Memphis, at the border between Lower and Upper Egypt. Memphis was to be the capital for many later "pharaohs," or kings. In the desert west of Memphis the third dynasty king Zoser (about 2780 B.C.) built a stepped stone pyramid, a tomb that rose in six stages to a height of 200 feet. Zoser's architect, Imhotep, who was also magician, wise man and physician, should perhaps be given credit for the later pyramids of the third and fourth dynasties, which must have been adapted from his original design.

At this time of consolidation, Egypt's foreign policy was concerned with making the frontiers secure, not with expansion. There was no organized army. Instead, each province had a local militia that could be called up in case of a serious threat.

Pepi I of the sixth dynasty did, however, gain power over the Nubians who lived near the first cataract of the Nile. He added Nubians to his troops

Below: Rameses II (12th century B.C.) on a campaign in Syria when it was part of the Hittite empire. As a god-king he is shown larger than his enemies. During his long reign, Rameses built a new capital at Tanis on the Nile delta and numerous temples, including the great rock temple at Abu Simbel.

Above: Nefertiti, famed for her beauty, was the wife of Iknaton. She greatly influenced her husband in the social, political, religious and artistic changes he made during his reign.

Throne of Tutankhamon, boy-king of ancient Egypt, dating from the 14th century B.C. The back of the throne, made of gold ornamented with silver and precious stones, shows the young king with his bride. The throne is now exhibited in the Cairo museum.

and then attacked the Bedouins, who had been raiding the eastern Delta. On this campaign the Egyptians traveled north to Palestine for the first time. Pepi II the next pharaoh, sent explorers deeper into the southern lands. One expedition brought back a much-valued pygmy from inner Africa as a gift to the pharaoh.

The Old Kingdom came to an end around 2300 B.C. after about 900 years of rule. Asian invaders moved into the Delta and the noble provincial families divided the pharaoh's power among themselves.

Pharaohs of the 11th dynasty reunited the country in about 2050 B.C. During the Middle Kingdom era, Egypt continued to control parts of Nubia and sent troops into Palestine and Syria, but her basic policy was still defensive. A fort was built to guard the eastern frontier, and Sesostris III (about 1887–1849 B.C.) built a fort on each side of the Nile to mark Egypt's southern boundary, just above the second cataract.

A serious invasion from Asia put an end to the Middle Kingdom. The invaders, called "Hyksos" (Shepherd Kings), poured into the Delta on horseback and in chariots, leaving ruined cities in their wake, destroying temples, enslaving women and children. They set themselves up as rulers and adopted many Egyptian ways. But Theban kings finally restored Egypt's unity, overcoming the aliens by 1570 B.C.

The New Kingdom, ancient Egypt's most powerful period, now began. An army was organized, and this time conquest was the aim. The 18th dynasty king Thutmose III (15th century B.C.) campaigned for 19 years and annexed Palestine, Syria, and Phoenicia into a great empire stretching 1,700 miles south from the Taurus Mountains to beyond the fourth cataract.

But the Hittites of Asia Minor attacked Syria during the reign of Amenophis IV (Iknaton) and his successors inherited the long struggle for the Asian lands. The Libyans became active in the west, moving against the Delta. In the north, the "peoples of the sea" migrated from the northern Mediterranean eastward, destroying the Hittite kingdom. Rameses II (about 1189–1157 B.C.) defeated the "peoples of the sea" about where the Suez Canal now runs, but by the end of the 12th century Egypt ceased to control her Asian dominions.

There was a resurgence during the 26th dynasty (about 650–550 B.C.). Before that, however, the fierce Assyrians had appeared more than once at Egypt's gates. Egypt was saved only by the fact that Assyria had more than enough worries in Asia. Then, in 525 B.C., the "black land" was finally conquered by Cambyses of Persia.

Everyday Life in Ancient Egypt

Papyrus painting of the god Anubis weighing a human heart against the feather of truth. He is often represented as a crouching jackal since this was his sacred animal. Anubis conducted souls to the underworld and judged men's good and bad deeds on earth.

Right: formal Egyptian hieroglyphics.
Far right: simplified hieratic script which was in everyday use.
Below: 3400-year-old wall painting shows that Egyptians recorded amounts of grain.

The civilization developed by the ancient Egyptians, and maintained for 3,000 years, was far in advance of their neighbors'. The Egyptians had two things in their favor: the life-giving Nile and the barriers of the Libyan and Arabian deserts to the west and east, which discouraged invasion.

Not that Egypt was isolated. The Nile was an avenue for trade and communication. In the south the Egyptians traded for gold, ivory, ebony, incense and panther skins. Lacking wood, they obtained it from Syria to the north. They mined copper in the Sinai Peninsula and traded with Crete, and in the Middle Kingdom era they built a canal connecting the Nile to the Red Sea. Trade was usually carried on by barter, but there were copper and gold rings that served as money. Taxes, however, were usually paid in grain or goods.

The majority of the population of several million were serfs, who farmed the lands of the nobles or of the temples. They harvested huge crops of wheat and barley, also growing vegetables, tending vineyards, and cultivating flax to be spun into linen cloth. They kept herds of sheep, cattle, goats, and donkeys—but no horses until after the Hyksos invasion. Every summer from July to September the Nile overflowed, irrigating the fields and depositing rich silt.

Egypt was basically an agricultural, feudal society, but the crafts were not neglected. Craftsmen, usually in the service of a lord or perhaps of the pharaoh himself, produced tools of bronze and copper, furniture, jewelry, leather goods, textiles.

Theoretically the pharaoh was the owner of all land, but actually a "house document" served as a deed, establishing ownership of property from generation to generation. As the office of provincial governor also became hereditary, the power of some of the noble landowners grew. They acted as local judges as well as administrators, and in some periods of Egyptian history ruled their provinces, or "nomes," independently. But the most important law cases went before the Great Kenbet, or high court, in the capital.

Left: tomb painting of a noble hunting wild birds in the Nile marshes. Using a snake-shaped stick to knock down the water fowl, he is standing in a light skiff made of papyrus.

Isis, goddess of motherhood and fertility, wife of Osiris, chief god of the underworld. She and Osiris were the only deities worshiped throughout Egypt. In her right hand Isis carries the *ankh* or emblem of life and her headdress is made of cow's horns and a sun disc.

A noble or wealthy man often had a harem. Only one woman was legally his wife, however, and her sons were his heirs. Women generally were respected and even could become queen, as did Hatshepsut (1504–1482 B.C.).

The pharaohs reigned with the help of a vizier and such officials as the tax collectors and the managers of the granite quarries and copper mines. The priests and scribes were also important to the pharaoh, sometimes exerting great power, because of their astronomy, mathematics and writing.

Papyrus reeds growing in the marshes were made into paper as early as the Old Kingdom period. Scribes wrote in ink on long rolls, some 100 feet long, often using an everyday script called "hieratic" rather than the more elaborate and formal hieroglyphs. Scholars learned to write at temple schools which taught both priests and laymen.

The Egyptian calendar of 365 days, already in use among the Delta Egyptians in the 43rd century B.C., was later adopted by Julius Caesar. The Egyptian numeral system was adequate for practical needs, but cumbersome: It took 27 figures to express the number 999.

Religion affected all aspects of life, and contributed to the stability of Egyptian civilization. There were strange creatures living in the Nile—crocodiles, hippopotamuses—and their images, along with the ibis (a wading bird), the jackal, the lion and the cow, were combined with human forms to portray the gods. Of more than 2,000 deities, the most important were Re, the sun god, Osiris, god of the underworld, Isis, goddess of motherhood. Priests upheld the pharaoh as a god-king. In the Old Kingdom men believed each living pharaoh was the son of Re and each dead pharaoh was Osiris. Magic was also practiced, generally to drive away evil spirits.

Their wall paintings depict the Egyptians as a pleasure-loving people. Although their religion placed greater emphasis on life after death than any other in ancient times, the Egyptians—or at least the pharaoh and nobles—expected to enjoy themselves after death.

15

Opposite page: pyramids at Giza. The Great Pyramid, in the center and more than 480 feet high, was built about 2600 B.C. by Pharaoh Khufu. Left: the Great Sphinx, also at Giza, guards a king's tomb. The sphinx, representing the god Horus, usually had a man's head and the body of a crouching lion.
Below: the second of Tutankhamon's three coffins, showing the young king's head. Over his brow are the heads of a vulture and a cobra, symbols of sovereignty.

Top: proto-Hittite stag dating from 2300–2100 B.C. found at Alacahöyük. This carving may have been an offering to Rutash, the Hittite goddess of hunting, or a representation of the goddess herself.
Left: eighth century B.C. sculpture of a Hittite king, from the Lion Gate at Malatya.

During the second half of the third millennium B.C. central Anatolia (modern Turkey) was the home of the Hatti, a people named after Hattusas (the present Boghazköy), their chief city. We know little of the Hatti, but it seems certain that they were not Hittites, with whom they have sometimes been wrongly identified. About 2000 B.C., they were conquered by the first wave of Hittites to flow into Anatolia—the proto-Hittites, also called the hieroglyphic Hittites, from their way of writing. These invaders were Indo-Europeans (p. 29) and may have come originally from the Caucasus region of southern Russia. Their capital, Kussura, was probably the modern Alacahöyük. Objects found at this important site, where excavation has also revealed traces of even earlier peoples, include bowls and copperware; gold and silver vases, and strange discs bearing swastikas; and small statues of stags, bulls and other animals—probably intended as offerings to Rutash, the Hittite goddess of hunting, or perhaps as representations of the goddess herself.

Early in the second millennium another wave of Hittites, the cuneiform Hittites, surged into Anatolia. First Kussura fell into their hands, and then a town called Nesas, which became their capital.

The Nesite kings were not lacking in ambition or aggression, essential attributes of early peoples wishing to survive. Hittite domination of all of

Anatolia, completed during the reign of Tlabarnis I (about 1680–1650 B.C.), was followed by the conquest of Haleb, a kingdom of north Syria, by Hattusilis I (1650–1620 B.C.), Tlabarnis' son, who ruled from Hattusas. With the sack of Babylon (p. 20) by Mursilis I (1620–1590 B.C.) Nesite power reached its zenith. But after the assassination of Mursilis what had been won was lost by the quarrels of rival princelings. For a time the once proud Hittite kingdom may even have been the subject territory of Mitanni, the powerful neighboring state of the Hurrians in northern Mesopotamia and Syria.

Unity and sense of purpose were restored by Tudhaliyas (1460–1440 B.C.) and after varying fortunes the new Hittite Empire entered its golden age—the reign of Suppiluliumas (1385–1335 B.C.), the greatest of the Hittite kings, victor over the Hurrians and conqueror of Azzi (Armenia). Many of the finest items from Boghazköy date from his reign and that of his successor, Mursilis II (1334–1306 B.C.).

Hittite expansion to the south was viewed by Egypt with increasing alarm. The two powers clashed in 1286 B.C. at Kadesh on the Orontes River in Syria. The battle seems to have been indecisive and a compromise peace was eventually arranged —perhaps because the Hittites themselves were now being threatened by other foes. Sea-going peoples were now moving into Anatolia, where existing groups were also on the move. The Hittite Empire was fractured by Phrygian and other pressures. Small Hittite kingdoms appeared in northern Syria, but these too disappeared in time. About 1000 B.C. the Arameans established city-state kingdoms in Asia Minor. These, however, were rarely united and were therefore easily conquered (about 700 B.C.) by the Assyrians (p. 22).

The Hittite monarchy was hereditary but not absolute. The accession of each "Great King" had to be approved by the Council of Nobles. Divinely inspired, the king was also high priest, the supreme interpreter of the will of the gods, who himself became a god when he died. As commander-in-chief of the army he maintained his own corps of professional soldiers, but could require his nobles to provide further troops in time of war. Below this upper crust of Hittite society came the majority of the people—the tradesmen, artisans, laborers and peasants. Lowest of all were the slaves. We know from finds at Boghazköy that the Hittites had elaborate legal codes; their laws were generally more humane than those of the Babylonians or Assyrians,

Hittite deities were associated with the forces of nature. Foremost was Arinna, the Great Goddess. "Queen of the land of Hatti," who was also known as Hepatu or Hebat. She both inspired and helped

Top: King's Gate, Boghazköy, site of Hattusas, the Hittite capital. Below: the god Sarumma embracing the young king Tudhaliyas IV, from a rock carving at Yazilikaya. The Hittite kings were also high priests; people believed they became gods after death.

the king. Her husband, the Great God, also known as Teshub, presided over the weather. Their children included the Sun God (Telepinu) and the goddess of medicine (Kamrusepa). Worship of these deities involved elaborate ceremony—ritual bathing, libations and the sacrifice of animals.

Convincing evidence that the Hittites were a cultured people at a more advanced stage of civilization than many of their neighbors is provided by their remarkably original and often surprisingly sophisticated art. Their poetry and other literature were also of a high order. These achievements suggest that their influence was probably much greater than historians once thought.

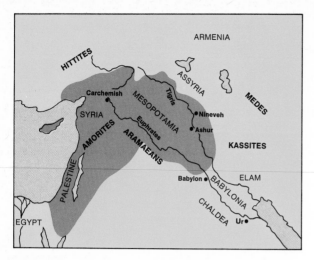

Top: map shows extent of the Assyrian Empire about 720 B.C.
Dominance of Mesopotamia (the land 'between rivers') alternated
between Babylonia and Assyria.
Below: Hammurabi's legal code inscribed on stone shaft.
Hammurabi himself is shown on the left, receiving his code from
the sun god Marduk, seated on his throne. Dating from the
1700s B.C., this is the oldest known law code.

The Babylonians

The rich lands of the Tigris-Euphrates plains had
always attracted invaders from desert and mountain. Mesopotamia had been a battleground for
centuries before the fall of the city of Ur (p. 8).

It was the Elamites who finally took Ur, but another group of invaders, the Amorites, were to be
more significant. Entering from the western deserts
in about 2000 B.C., these Semitic nomads pitched
their tents all across the divided country, sometimes
occupying towns. The Amorite town of Babylon,
at first a small kingdom, became the center of a
new empire under its sixth king, the great Hammurabi (about 1728–1686 B.C.). Babylonians grew
prosperous through commerce and trade, following
business practices like standard weights and measures, legal agreements, lending money at interest
rates and even flood insurance.

Sumerian gods had already been adopted by the
Babylonians, and Hammurabi wisely built on the
Sumerian culture in other areas—architecture,
government, commerce. Even his famous code of
laws had been preceded by a Sumerian system.

Nevertheless Hammurabi's Code was a notable
achievement. Over a thousand years would elapse
before the Romans would surpass it. The Code
divided the people into three groups: nobles and
landowners, slaves, and a middle group who were
poor but might own a slave or some land. Punish-
ments for offenses varied according to status. For
example, a man who had put out the eye of a noble
was blinded himself, but he only had to pay a fine
if his victim had been a poor man or a slave. Though
penalties were often severe—mutilation or death—
the basis of this justice was to protect the weak.

Near the end of Hammurabi's long reign, he
defeated Assyria and adopted the title "King of the
Four Quarters of the World." His successors, however, had trouble holding Hammurabi's empire.
The cities within his realm revolted and Kassites
and Hittites made inroads from outside, carving
more and more off the country. A destructive Hittite raid (about 1594 B.C.) dealt the deathblow to
the 300-year-old Babylonian dynasty.

Babylonia was now to be conquered by Kassites.
These highlanders from the east, though semi-
barbaric, behaved strangely like other kings of
Mesopotamia in their 400 years of rule: rebuilding
temples and canals, and maintaining an organized
political life.

Standing out against a blue-enamelled brick background, one of the many bulls that made the Ishtar Gate Babylon an impressive sight. The Ishtar Gate arched over a broad road used for magnificent processions. Babylon's inner wall with its many bronze gates was surrounded by a moat. The giant ziggurat inside the city inspired the "Tower of Babel" story.

The Kassites had been overthrown by Elamites for some centuries when Assyria defeated Babylonia in 721 B.C., keeping it a subject nation until 626 B.C. In that year the land was liberated by the Chaldeans, who had first invaded southern Babylonia around 1100 B.C. Babylonia once again became a great state under the Chaldean ruler Nabopolassar. His son Nebuchadnezzar II (605–562 B.C.) extended Chaldean power, defeating the Egyptian king Necho at Carchemish in 605 B.C. and taking Jerusalem twice.

Babylon had always been a center of trade. Now it became the greatest, most magnificent city in the Near East. Its outer wall was so extensive (11 miles long) that 200,000 people could be contained within it and so wide (80 feet) that a chariot could turn around on top. The inner wall had eight gates. The northwestern gate, named for the goddess Ishtar, was particularly impressive—35 feet high with 70-foot towers rising on each side and decorated in relief by colored figures of bulls and dragons.

Mesopotamian literature and astronomy continued to develop. Chaldean priests could even predict eclipses of the sun and moon after making careful observations of the "roads" of the sun and planets.

During this creative period, no one gave particular thought to the vassals of the Medes, known as Persians. Babylonia's last independent king, Nabonidus, has been nicknamed "the royal archeaologist" because of his passionate interest in studying the past. But in the future was Cyrus, the Persian who took Babylon in 539 B.C., only 87 years after the new Babylonian dynasty had begun (p. 109).

Right: Babylonian bronze statue (about 1000 B.C.) of Pazuzu. This demon is a personification of the scorching desert wind that brought storm and fever.
Below: Arbela (modern Erbil, Iraq) in northeast Mesopotamia. This town had been established for more than 1000 years when Hammurabi launched his attack on Assyria about 1850 B.C. The close-packed houses, protective wall and fertile strips of the present day town echo the living pattern of ancient Arbela.

Eighth century B.C. figure of
Gilgamesh from Khorsabad.
The epic of Gilgamesh, from
Babylonian literature, is a
narrative poem about the
mythical king of Erech, who
was half man, half god.

The Assyrians, a Semitic people living in north-eastern Mesopotamia, derived their name from Ashur, the city around which they settled in about 2000 B.C. (map p. 20). Even though their kingdom was small and infertile, they were under constant attack from such powerful Mesopotamian leaders as Sargon of Akkad and Hammurabi of Babylonia, from the warlike peoples of the mountains looming to the east, from Hittites, and even from Egyptians.

It is not surprising, therefore, that the Assyrians developed from peasant farmers into a nation dedicated to war and bloodshed.

The Assyrian army was highly organized, divided into squads of 10 men with 5 to 20 squads making up a company. Cavalry and chariot maneuvers were part of carefully planned military strategies. For besieging cities and towns, the Assyrians built formidable platforms on wheels, so high that archers could fire down on the defenders of a walled city and they used rams reinforced with iron to smash in gates and walls.

By the ninth century B.C. Assyrian aggressiveness and military skill began to reap rewards. Ashurnasirpal II (883–858 B.C.) led the Assyrian army against an old enemy, the Arameans to the west, and then marched all the way to the Mediterranean to demand, and get, tribute from Phoenician cities. He and his successors treated their enemies cruelly, often impaling them and burning them alive.

Siege of a city (884 B.C.) showing part of the efficient Assyrian war machine with (center) a large battering ram.

Reconstruction of the palaces of Nimrud. The Assyrian army headquarters, Nimrud was a new city built by Shalmaneser I.

Assyrian expansion continued throughout the ninth century, and, in the eighth, Tiglath-pileser III and Sargon II took Babylonia, Syria, and Israel; Sargon taking 10 of the 12 tribes of Israel as captives. When Babylon revolted in 689 B.C., Sennacherib, Sargon's son, spared neither city nor inhabitants. Much of the city was rebuilt by Esarhaddon, the next Assyrian king, as atonement for the evil done by his father.

The policy of deporting conquered populations was one way in which the Assyrians maintained their power. In some conquered lands Assyrian governors were installed as rulers. Other subject nations continued to rule themselves but had to pay tribute. Often an Assyrian official stayed in a foreign court, more a spy than a diplomat. The Assyrian king also decided who would hold office in all of his provinces, and a system of roads was constructed so that he could get the latest news from all over his empire.

The Assyrians always seem to be in the field, hunting if not actually in battle. Nevertheless, they did absorb the cultures of those they defeated, particularly that of Babylonia. Ashurbanipal (669–631 B.C.) was a patron of the arts as well as a warring king. He collected a library of over 22,000 cuneiform tablets, many of them copies of ancient Sumerian and Babylonian works.

Although the Assyrians were mainly copyists in the field of literature, in stone sculpture they produced masterpieces. Palace gates were guarded by massive carvings of winged bulls and lions with human heads. Assyrian reliefs are strong, realistic scenes, and, characteristically, depict war or hunting much more frequently than religious events. Sennacherib, Babylon's destroyer, was a builder as well, restoring Nineveh, a very old city on the east bank of the Tigris (opposite the modern Mosul) that he made the capital. His palace was magnificent; an aqueduct and a 30-mile-long canal built to irrigate Nineveh's botanical garden and surrounding fields, were marvels of engineering.

Assyrian power was at its height during Ashurbanipal's reign. After his death, the empire might have survived the Chaldean revolt in Babylonia if the Medes had not suddenly attacked from the northeast. Assyria, threatened on two sides, even asked Egypt for help. But in 612 B.C. Nineveh was destroyed, the dreaded Assyrian warriors killed or scattered, and the empire had fallen.

Huge winged bull with human head guarding the gates of the Khorsabad palace of King Sargon II. Although only one storey high, the palace had many imposing rooms and courtyards.

Busy trading scene from sixth century Spartan drinking cup. King Arcesilaus of Cyrene in North Africa presides over the weighing of export produce. One of the city's main exports was sylphium, a "pep" drug used by the priestesses of the oracles. Founded as an Hellenic colony in the seventh century B.C., Cyrene came under Persian domination in the sixth century, Alexandrian in the fourth century and eventually under the rule of Rome in 95 B.C. The city was most prosperous under the Emperor Trajan when the population numbered 100,000. Its great wealth came from exporting huge quantities of grain to Italy. Today Cyrene is only a small village.

THE AEGEAN

We now move from the Near and Middle East to the eastern Mediterranean, whose many islands and indented coasts saw the rise of two great cultures, the Cretan and the Greek. The isolation imposed by sea and mountain favored the growth of city-states and, in their citizens, the development of a highly independent and keenly reasoning outlook. From the Greeks came democracy, philosophy, and enduring contributions to the arts and sciences. Their achievements still influence our way of life

Minoan Crete

The first European civilization began about 5,000 years ago on the island of Crete. No great river flowed through this fertile mountainous island. In this Crete differed from those other centers of early civilization—Egypt, the Indus Valley and Mesopotamia. All had built prosperity upon their fertile river valleys. But Crete had no need of any such rivers. Instead there was the Mediterranean Sea itself, a more expansive road to wealth and power.

The people of ancient Crete—short, slender, dark-haired, and skilled in using bronze—are usually called "Minoans," after the legendary Cretan king Minos. Just where they came from is unclear. They may have been migrants from northern Africa, though some historians have suggested that their ancestors had some kind of connection with the Hittites of Asia Minor.

Excavations on the island began in 1900 under the direction of the British archaeologist Arthur Evans. Under other archaeologists they are still going on, for Crete is an archaeological paradise. Evans, though, probably unearthed both of the island's richest jewels. The two most important sites are the cities of Knossos, near the northern shore, and Phaestus, near the southern. In both places magnificent palaces attest to the high level of culture in Crete between 2500 and 1400 B.C.

The palace at Knossos with its spendid throne room, halls and stairways and large storage chambers, lends credence to a Greek legend about the Greek hero Theseus, who slew the Minotaur, a monstrous bull-man living in a labyrinth. Until Evans made his startling discoveries, this legend had been dismissed for many years as merely good storytelling; but the plan of the corridors, rooms, and courts of the palace more closely resembles a labyrinth than anything yet discovered from ancient times. And the Minoans' sacred regard for the bull is manifest in statuettes and paintings.

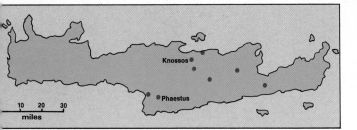

Map of Crete shows location of eight cities founded between 3000 and 2000 B.C. About 2000 B.C. the islanders were united under one or more rulers. From 1600 B.C. Cretans began trading with other Mediterranean ports.

The work of the Cretan stonemasons and engineers—evident in their stairways and sanitation drains, for example—is equalled by that of other early civilizations. In their frescoes and pottery, however, the Minoans excelled, expressing their love of bright colors and swirling shapes.

The tales depicted on walls and vases, are rarely of battles or sieges, but of dancing and feasting, of people celebrating a harvest or fearlessly leaping over the horns of a bull in a strange religious ritual. The women could almost be fashion models with their full skirts tight at the waist, jewelry on their necks and arms, and the men, too, obviously took pains with their appearance. In paintings and pottery such denizens of the sea as the octopus and dolphin recur, along with designs based on plants and birds. Their vivid realism speaks plainly of the keen observation by Minoan artists of the living things around them. Tools and ornaments are decorated by gold and ivory inlay with the same painstaking attention to detail as artists devoted to Minoan paintings.

Unlike their Mycenaean contemporaries on the mainland of Greece, the Minoans did not fortify their palaces or towns against invasion. Who could attack them by sea when they controlled it? During the high period of Cretan history, these expert sailors made the Mediterranean and Aegean seas their dominions. They sailed south to Egypt, trading olive oil and pottery for delicate alabaster vases and other Egyptian goods; east to Asia; north to the Aegean world, taking metalwork and vases to the Greek mainland, only 60 miles away. And when the Minoans landed with their wares they evidently brought political power to bear. According to legend Athens and other Aegean cities were obliged to pay tribute to Crete at this time.

Some day we may learn more about the Minoans by reading the scripts they inscribed on clay tablets. Two scripts have been found, both with a sign for each syllable. The earlier is called "Linear A," the later, "Linear B." Linear A is still undeciphered, but the puzzle of Linear B was solved by an English architect, Michael Ventris, in 1951. Consisting of 90 signs, this language proved to be an ancient form of Greek and was used for inventories and other records. Although Ventris' discovery was a breakthrough, it did not clear up the one great mystery about Crete: the sudden destruction of the Minoan palaces in 1400 B.C.

We can only guess at the cause of the abrupt collapse of the elegant Minoan civilization. It could have been an earthquake, or it could have been that invasion by sea so little feared by the Minoans. Just at this time the Mycenaean Greeks were challenging their neighbors on land and Cretan power on the sea (p. 28). A Mycenaean invasion of the island could very well be the solution to the riddle.

Interior of the palace, Knossos. The walls (built of stone, rubble and sun-dried brick framed with wooden beams) were plastered and then decorated with paintings. The interior columns were inverted tree trunks set on ornamental stone bases, and these, too, were plastered and often decorated with concave, convex or spiral flutings.

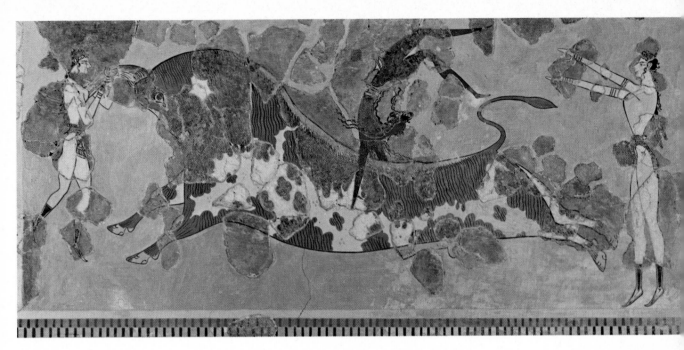

Top: fresco of man leaping over a bull, a dangerous sport of the Minoans and possible source of the Greek legend about Theseus and the Minotaur. This mural in the palace at Knossos is just one of the many paintings and carvings of bulls found in the town.

Left: throne room at Knossos. Behind the alabaster throne and benches are painted griffins and flowers. The priest-king often wore a crown of lilies since the lily was the sacred flower of Crete. The king's power was absolute; each year he announced the laws to his people.

Above: Linear B, an ancient Cretan script, used at Knossos for record keeping. Linear A, an older script than Linear B, was probably influenced by Egyptian hieorglyphics.

Right: dolphin fresco in the Queen's *megaron,* or hall, at the palace of Knossos. The furnishings of the royal suite were probably as elegant as the wall paintings, fine architecture and ornaments.

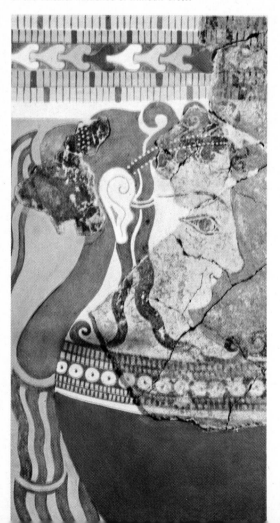

The Achaeans

During the second millennium B.C. tribes of people from the north were on the move, looking for a place to settle in southeastern Europe. They crossed the Balkan Mountains in waves: Arcadians first, followed by Achaeans, Ionians, Boeotians, Dorians, Illyrians, and Thracians.

These tribes spoke an Indo-European language which was to develop into Greek, and they were familiar with the superiority of bronze over stone for weapons and tools. Moving south into the plains of Greece, the tall, fair-skinned immigrants soon dominated the dark-haired people there.

Centuries later, after 1600 B.C., the Achaean Greeks in the Peloponnesus, the southern peninsula, could no longer be thought of merely as farmers or warriors from the savage north. They had learned to build walled fortified centers, with palaces and vaulted tombs.

The first evidence of this ancient Greek civilization was unearthed by the German archaeologist Heinrich Schliemann in 1876. The site was Mycenae where excavations revealed ancient royal graves dug as shafts into the hill. In each grave several bodies were laid one above the other. Buried with the bodies were many skillfully wrought objects: gold cups, goblets, masks, and ornaments, decorated swords and daggers. Much of the work seemed obviously Minoan—if not actually carried out by Minoan artists, it was certainly copied from their work. Other objects were products of a new and different culture. The scenes of war and hunting carved on stone steles marking the graves, for instance, were original in workmanship as well as choice of subject.

These early royal graves lay outside the walls of the palace-fort at first. Then in about 1400 B.C., the citadel was enlarged. The Lion Gate, an entrance in the new wall, is still standing. So is the "Treasury of Atreus" (or "Tomb of Agamemnon"), the largest of the huge, vaulted, beehive-shaped tombs that were cut into the side of the hill outside the walls. No vault as large as the Treasury of Atreus was to be built again until the time of the Roman Empire.

In times of trouble, the defenders of Mycenae were able to hold out against long sieges, because they had plenty of water. Inside the walls 93 steps went down to a well deep in the hillside.

Mycenae became the most powerful of the

Above: the Lion Gate, entrance to the citadel of Mycenae, dates from the 14th century B.C. when the town was enlarged.
Below: fragment of a fresco in the palace at Tiryns. The girl's hair style resembles those in Cretan wall paintings, an indication of the cultural influence of Minoan Crete.

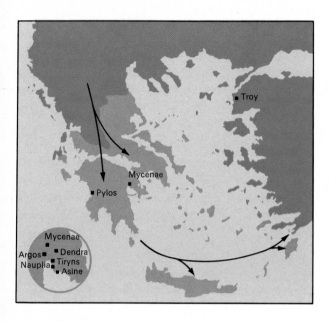

Arrows show possible invasion routes of Indo-European people between 2000 and 1000 B.C. Most present day European languages derive from Indo-European tongues. Pale area shows Homeric Greece. Inset are the centers of Mycaean power.

Vessels of Thracian gold. Thrace, whose mountains had valuable gold and silver deposits, stretched north from Macedonia to the Danube River. The Thracians, Indo-European people like the Greeks, were probably the allies of Priam, the last king of Troy.

Achaean fortified towns between 1400 and 1200 B.C.; its rulers controlled more of Greece than any subsequent leaders for 800 years. Most Mycenaean centers—Mycenae, Tiryns, Argos, Dendra, Asine, Nauplia, Pylos—were on or close to the sea, and these Greeks developed a talent for piracy, raiding weaker ships and islands in the Aegean Sea. The dominance of Crete had been destroyed in 1400, perhaps by the Mycenaeans themselves. With Crete no longer a power to contend with, Mycenaean confidence grew. Early in the 12th century B.C. they attacked the wealthy city of Troy.

The united Achaeans, their fleet led by Agamemnon—King of Mycenae, Tiryns, and Argos—are traditionally said to have besieged this old city on the coast of Asia Minor for 10 years (1194–1184 B.C.). The victory over Troy came in a period when Achaean power was at its peak. Homer's epic poem, the *Iliad*, is set against the background of this war.

In Homer's version, the abduction of Helen, the most beautiful woman in the world, by young Paris of Troy started the Trojan war. Helen was the wife of Menelaus, the Achaean king of Sparta, and the other Achaean rulers were pledged to support Menelaus in his grievance. A great poetic imagination makes the *Iliad* exciting to readers today, but the work is a tale of the ways of heroes and gods, not a historical record. It was written 300 years or more after the actual events. Even so, archaeological findings do support some of the detail in Homer's account.

Two other famous epics are concerned with the aftermath of the Trojan war: Homer's *Odyssey*, which describes the adventures of Odysseus on his homeward journey from Troy; and the *Aeneid*, by the much later Latin poet Vergil, which tells about the Trojans who escaped from their defeated city.

The Mycenaean period certainly gave rise to heroic legends. But it came to a sudden, unheroic end. About 1100 B.C. the Dorian Greeks swarmed south into the Peloponnesus and overwhelmed the Mycenaean world, taking Mycenae and Pylos, making serfs, or *helots*, of the Spartans, intermarrying with both pre-Greeks and the Greeks already there. Only Attica the smaller peninsula northeast of the Peloponnesus was lucky; when the Dorians moved down from central Greece, they went south across the Gulf of Corinth instead of turning east.

For several centuries Greeks lived in a Dark Age, a time of violence and chaos.

29

Colonies of Greece

Map legend:
- ■ Milesian cities
- ● Euboean cities
- ▲ Phocaean cities
- ■ Corinthian cities
- ● Various Greek cities
- ▲ Phoenician cities

Map shows Greek and Phoenician colonies on the Mediterranean, Aegean and Black Seas. Greek mother cities are indicated by large symbols, the colonies they established by smaller symbols. Solid circles show other cities founded by Greek emigrants. This expansion was due partly to the shortage of good farmland in Greece.

The Dorian invasions set off a chain reaction of emigration from mainland Greece (1200–900 B.C.). In their southward thrusts, the Dorians eventually colonized the islands of Melos, Crete, Rhodes, and Cos and the shores of southwest Asia Minor. And as the Dorians advanced, many pre-Dorian Greeks fled across the Aegean to Cyprus and Asia Minor. And of those who remained, most found themselves working as serfs for Dorian overlords.

But the Dorians contributed more to the history of Greece than just another chapter in its military history. They added to its material progress too.

The Dorians brought iron into Greece. Iron hoes and plows prepared the stony earth for seed far better than the tools of the Bronze Age. The population expanded along with the growth of food production. By 800 B.C. the peasant population had grown tremendously; but their farms had shrunk as the nobles, mostly Dorian, appropriated more and more land for their own estates. Soon the Greek farmer preferred taking his chances in strange country to starving at home. In a new land he might

even do so well that he or his sons could become nobles themselves. Thus, by shipping out the discontented, the city-states avoided revolution, and at the same time gained new sources for grain, a vital commodity.

Fear of attack had sparked off the first great wave of emigration from Greece. Fear of hunger prompted the next one. This second exodus, moving far beyond the Aegean, began in 750 B.C. For centuries Greek sailors had been thoroughly at home in the waters of the Aegean, grateful for the many islands and coastal inlets that offered shelter in a storm. Now they ventured over the open sea, first across the Mediterranean west to Italy, Sicily, Corsica, Sardinia and south to the coast of Africa; later into the Black Sea and the fertile lands along its southern and southeast coasts.

Sometimes two city-states combined forces and sent out a joint expedition of settlers. Eretria and Chalcis on Euboea were partners in founding Cumae on Italy's western shore. This was the first Greek colony in the west. Sicily also attracted the Euboean coalition, soon imitated by Corinth, Rhodes, and Megara. Of all the Sicilian colonies, Corinth's Syracuse, founded by the nobleman Archias in 734 B.C. became the most impressive city. It had become the capital of *tyrants* (p. 32) by the fifth century B.C.; and its population grew to 250,000 by the fourth, far outstripping its mother city. From Asia Minor Phocaea sent colonists all the way to what is now France, establishing Massilia (Marseille) and other settlements. Sparta founded Tarentum in southern Italy.

Each Greek city was independent, so the colonies they established did not make up an empire. Nor was a colony politically dependent on the mother city, though it was natural enough that there should be ties of loyalty and commerce.

Although the need for land had been the original spur to colonization in 750 B.C., an inevitable growth of trade contributed in turn to further colonization. In a new surge of emigration beginning in the seventh century B.C. more than 90 colonies were established around the Black Sea, by Greek

The Tholos, part of the ruins at Delphi. High up on the southern slopes of Mount Parnassus, Delphi was sacred to the ancient Greeks. They dedicated the site to the god Apollo and built a temple, theater, stadium and other monuments.

Temple of Poseidon at Paestum near Salerno, Italy, built about 450 B.C. Founded about 600 B.C. by Achaean colonists from Sybaris, Paestum was a flourishing town by 540 B.C.

cities in Asia Minor and by Megara. By 600 B.C. Greek colonies spread from Spain to the eastern-most shore of the Black Sea, a span of more than 2,000 miles.

Mainland Greece came to depend on the colonies for raw materials: first grain, then such imports as timber, metal and fruit. The mainland exported oil, wine and manufactures. The quality of Greek exports improved, bringing Greeks into intensive competition with Phoenicia for the trade of such peoples as the Scythians around the Black Sea, the Berbers of North Africa, the Celts in France.

The Semitic Phoenicians of the eastern Mediterranean coast had been expert navigators and traders for a long time. After the fall of the Cretan sea kings, Phoenician ships had sailed north to the Black Sea and west into the open Atlantic. Utica, probably their oldest colony in Africa, had been settled about

1100 B.C., Carthage in 814. People there did not welcome the arrival in their own private trading ground of shipload after shipload of adventurous aggressive Greeks.

In about 580 B.C. Greeks attacked the Phoenician strong points of western Sicily. Even before that the colonists at Massilia had clashed with Phoenicians. Carthage, with colonies of her own, responded by organizing other Phoenician cities into an anti-Greek alliance, and enlisting the Etruscans in Italy. In 535 B.C. they won a naval battle that forced the Greeks to withdraw from Corsica. The conflict dragged on.

It was still an undecided issue 300 years later when the Romans drove the Carthaginians from Sicily (p. 46). The Greek colonists there, and in other places were fated to be absorbed by Roman expansion.

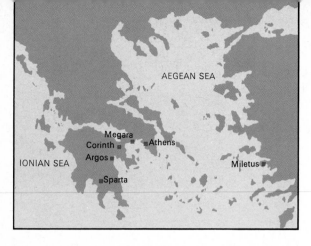

AEGEAN SEA

Megara
Corinth
Athens
Argos
IONIAN SEA
Miletus
Sparta

Map shows Greek city centers named in text. Revolutions in the seventh and sixth centuries shook these city-states, as they did other independent cities. Power began shifting from the aristocrats to the champions of the people or "tyrants." However, the Dorian rulers of Sparta succeeded in crushing peasant revolts in their city-state.

As ancient Greece left the Dark Age and expanded, it came to consist of hundreds of independent city-states on the mainland, on the Aegean islands, along the Asia Minor shore, dotted all around the Mediterranean and Black Sea. Greece was not a united country, not a political empire, but groups of people loosely unified by language, trade and religion.

The geography of the mainland encouraged the independence of the city-states. Each fertile plain was cut off from the others, with mountains rising all round, most often with the sea as a barrier on one side.

Most towns developed at the base of an *acropolis*, or "high city," a fortress built on the most easily defended hill, near enough to the fields so farmers could retreat to it quickly with their herds in times of danger.

In Mycenaean times, the citadel had also been the residence of the king (p. 28). After the Dark Age, nearly all the kings were replaced by councils of aristocrats, and the fortress became the place for assembly and worship. The town built up outside the walls. Farmers brought their produce to the town's market and bartered for the wares of local craftsmen, for the imported goods of the merchants, for the catch of the fishermen.

The city-states were modest in size, populations ranging from less than 5,000 to 20,000. In Attica, where many small city-states were united under the leadership of Athens, the free population in the fifth century B.C. did reach 250,000. The colony of Syracuse on the island of Sicily also grew this large. But these were exceptions. Sparta, the largest city-state in area, was not much bigger than the island of Crete—3,300 square miles.

By 800 B.C. most city-states were governed by the wealthy, landowning nobles, Ionians or descendants of the Dorians (p. 29) who had crushed the local kings. They had little regard for the rights of the peasants, taking their best land, denying them a voice in the government, passing arbitrary judgment on them. Sending peasants out as colonists temporarily relieved some of the revolutionary pressure that was building up. Then, as trade increased because of the colonies, a new middle class without land—the traders and craftsmen—also began to resent aristocratic policies. In the seventh century B.C. rebellions threatened the old order of oligarchic rule by the few.

The results were greatly helped by artisan troops, the foot soldiers who had followed the aristocratic cavalry in inter-city wars. So they were already trained, experienced in fighting side by side, the

Vase painting of Greek charioteer driving twin-horse team. Although the cavalry and charioteers were noblemen, the heavily armed hoplite infantry made up of artisans was the pivot of defense. This importance gave impetus to the rise of a middle class.

The tyrant Peisistratus enhanced the beauty of Athens by fostering the arts. In this restful vase painting, women draw water from the Enneacrounos or "nine-mouthed" fountain. A reservoir supplied the water which flowed from sculptured spouts.

shield of one guarding the right side of the man to his left. They were called *hoplites* or "weapon bearers" because they supplied their own arms—helmets, shields, armor, swords and spears.

In almost every Greek city, the ruling aristocrats were ousted as other aristocrats led the hoplites against them. The new leaders were given the name "tyrants," a word that meant "lord" or "chief" at this time without implying cruel misuse of power. Some of the most famous tyrants were Cypselus and his son Periander in Corinth (about 650–580 B.C.), Theagenes in Megara (about 640 B.C.), Thrasybulus in Miletus (about 600 B.C.), and Peisistratus in Athens (about 561 B.C.).

As leaders of popular revolt, the successful tyrants made concessions to the people. Coined money was now in use, an idea imported from Lydia in Asia Minor. The tyrants spent tax money on building temples of stone instead of wood as before. They courted popularity by promoting festivals, encouraging the arts and constructing public works.

A tyranny did not usually last through the rule of the second generation. The sons of tyrants tended to assume their right to power without paying attention to the will of the people. They became tyrants in the modern sense of the word, causing a new outburst of revolutions in the sixth century B.C.

Attica moved toward democracy. Corinth became an oligarchy once more under the rule of the leading families. Democracy and oligarchy alternated in fifth-century Argos.

Only the Dorian rulers of Sparta succeeded in maintaining some governmental stability, in spite of attempted revolts by *helots*, or serfs. Only Sparta had a standing army, consisting of citizens whose farms were tended by the helots. In the eighth century, this military-minded city-state had annexed Messenia, her neighbor to the west. In the sixth century, she used her army to back up an anti-tyrant policy, helping rebels of other cities to get rid of these rulers.

But of all the Greek city-states, it was fifth-century Athens, whose civilization soared the highest.

Painting on an ancient vase depicts battle scene of Greek against Greek. The infantry, protected by vizored helmets, greaves and shields, fight with swords and long spears.

Athens and Democracy

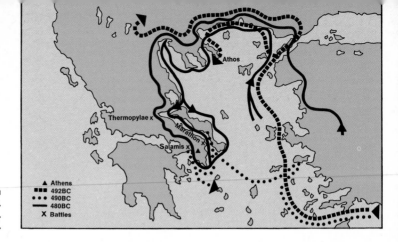

Map shows routes taken by Persian land and sea forces in 492 B.C. (square dots), 490 B.C. (round dots) and 480 B.C. (solid lines). Battles are marked by X.

▲ Athens
■■■ 492BC
●●● 490BC
━━━ 480BC
X Battles

The unification of Attica before 700 B.C. gives the first hint of Athens' future greatness. Unlike the Spartans in Messenia (p. 33), Athenians did not conquer and make serfs of their neighbors. Unification was a peaceful reorganization, with the free populations of the city-states of Attica becoming citizens of Athens.

In the seventh century B.C. Athens was ruled by nine *archons*. These magistrates were elected each year by a council of nobles, the *Areopagus*, which as time passed consisted of ex-archons.

The first tyrant to try to stir the people against the injustices of the nobles' rule failed to find enough support. But later the peasants found themselves burdened with ever-increasing debts, aggravated by the introduction of money instead of bartered goods as the major medium of exchange. They were starving and sometimes were even forced to become slaves, while the rich grew still richer. Yet Athens did not send her poor out to a colony as other city-states did. Her solution was unique. And it owed a great deal to the reforms conceived and put into motion by one man.

A merchant named Solon had written straightforward poetry about the greed of the wealthy. In 594 B.C. all factions agreed to let Solon, with the powers of a dictator, try to save a deteriorating situation. His program included cancelling all debts and freeing those enslaved for nonpayment of debts. Recognizing the inability of Attica to grow enough grain, he promoted the export of olive oil and pottery and the import of grain. He modified the laws, eliminating distinctions between rich and poor in their application. He set up an assembly of free male citizens who had veto power over a higher legislative council of 400. The requirements for becoming an archon were also liberalized, property rather than birth determining eligibility.

The tyrant Peisistratus (about 561 B.C.) upheld Solon's reforms. In addition, he loaned money to peasants and gave them the land of his opponents. He encouraged trade and industry, and attacked hereditary priesthoods—a source of power for the nobles—by favoring the popular Dionysian cult.

In 508 B.C. Cleisthenes made it harder than ever for the nobles to oppress the people by reforming the constitution and by setting up a council of 500. These three sixth-century statesmen paved the way for Athens' golden age, enabling Pericles (about 460 B.C.), as leader of the popular party, to consolidate democratic gains.

While the Athenians became freer, Greek cities

Top: Greek peasant with ox-drawn plow. Only half the fields were cultivated each year, the remainder were left fallow to regain some fertility.

Left: this type of wide-mouthed pot dating from the sixth or fifth century B.C. was called a krater. Potters making similar vessels are shown in red against a black background. Peisistratus encouraged this kind of industry and such red figure-ware helped make Athenian pottery a profitable export from the sixth century.

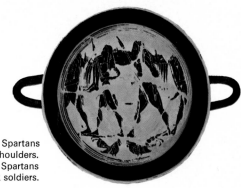

Cup of the sixth century B.C. shows Spartans bearing a battle casualty on their shoulders. Trained for war from an early age, the Spartans were the most disciplined of Greek soldiers.

in Asia Minor had yielded their independence to the Persians by 540 B.C. (p. 109). In 499 B.C. these Greek cities revolted. Athens sent 20 ships to their aid; Eretria, on Euboea, five. Darius I, the Persian ruler, crushed the rebellion and then decided to advance against European Greece, with Athens and Eretria as his main targets.

The Persians chose a route around the Aegean, 600 ships sailing parallel to the army's land advance. Their army had penetrated into Macedonia when a storm off Mount Athos destroyed half the fleet, ending the expedition. Two years later, in 490 B.C., Darius tried again, sending his forces straight across the Aegean. Eretria was taken, its temples razed and people enslaved. This hardened Athenian resistance. Though outnumbered two to one, the Athenians defeated 20,000 Persians at the famous battle of Marathon.

In 480 B.C., Xerxes, Darius' successor, mounted a third invasion, by way of Macedonia as in 492. Victory for the Greek alliance seemed impossible against a Persian army of about 200,000 and the large Persian fleet. At the pass at Thermopylae, 300 Spartans fought a hopeless battle. The Athenians had moved back to the island of Salamis when the Persians swept into Attica, burning the Acrop-olis at Athens. Then Themistocles, the Athenian leader, led the smaller Greek navy against the Persian fleet. The Persians lost 200 ships, the Greeks only 40. It was a proud day for Athens, the beginning of the end for Persian ambitions.

Athens now took the lead in driving the Persians not only from the mainland but from other Greek cities of the Aegean world. She made herself head of a league that more and more fell under her control. Her allies became the subjects of an Athenian Empire.

As her imperialism grew more forceful, Athens made some bitter enemies, particularly Sparta, leader of a rival league of Peloponnesian city-states. The Peloponnesian War between the two leagues began in 431 B.C. and continued until 404 when Athens capitulated. Her walls were torn down, her navy surrendered, her empire became only a memory.

Below left: detail from fourth century B.C. krater depicts Persian Emperor Darius (seated). After battles with the Greeks in Asia Minor, his army invaded the Greek mainland but was defeated at the Battle of Marathon in 490 B.C. Darius died in 486 B.C. while preparing a new attack on Greece.
Below: men shaking olive branches to dislodge the fruit. Most farmers in ancient Greece also grew wheat, barley and grapes.

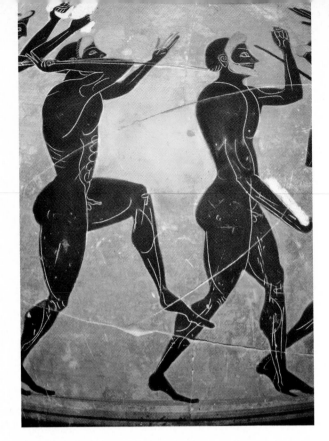

Competitors in the Panathenaic Games strive to win the pentathlon, an all-round test of athletic skill and stamina involving five events—running, jumping, wrestling, throwing the javelin and the discus. These games were held in honor of the goddess Athena.

Ancient Greek theater at Epidaurus. Its round orchestra or "dancing place" was one of the world's first stages. This theater seating 14,000 people has excellent acoustics. A music and drama festival is still held here every summer.

Everyday Life in a City-State

An Athenian of the fifth and fourth centuries B.C. had a way of life very different from that of modern society. His city, small enough for him to know it on foot, was like an accessible mountain, exhilarating but possible to climb in a day.

A man of moderate means lived in a small, windowless stone house built around an inner court so that it enclosed its occupants protectively. He got up at dawn and walked to his shop or workshop. Later in the day he strolled to the *agora*, or market place, to meet friends.

His wife rarely left the walled-in world of her house, not even to go to market. Her husband did the shopping, letting a slave carry his purchases. She stayed indoors and tended to linens, the making of cloth, the preparation and storage of food. She managed the household slaves and instructed her daughters in how to run a home.

Girls were raised from the start to accept a life of domestic isolation and a marriage arranged by their parents. But boys were educated for the more active part that they would play. They were taught to read and write an alphabet adapted from a Semitic alphabet brought from Phoenicia centuries before. They studied poetry, geometry, music and gymnastics. Perhaps the most useful thing a boy could learn was the art of speaking, for when he was older he would participate directly in Athens' political life. But only the wealthy could afford to pay the fees of the Sophists, who were the teachers of oratory.

The Athenian citizen was automatically a voting member of the all-powerful assembly. By the fourth century B.C. the once-powerful archons were elected by this body of free men and paid by the state. Citizens, chosen annually by lot, formed most of the government service and were generally paid for their work. Citizens chosen by lot also served on the world's first juries.

As a member of the assembly, a citizen could vote and speak on the measures submitted by the council of 500. He could offer his own proposals as well. In later times the conscientious citizen who attended a meeting of the assembly was even paid for his time. To the Athenian citizen, such involvement in the process of democracy was an essential part of being a free man. He did not turn the work over to a professional and let it go at that.

To some extent the institution of slavery—that ancient way of dealing with enemies defeated in war—made it possible for the Athenians to devote time to politics. A wealthy man might have as many as 1,000 slaves; a tradesman, one or two. Except for

Left: a follower of Dionysus performs a ritual dance. Such women devotees of the god were known as maenads. Right: oil jug decorated with the graceful figure of a muse playing the cithara, a lyre-like instrument. The nine muses were goddesses who patronized music, poetry, drama and other arts.

mineworkers, slaves of the Greeks had a much better life than they were later to have under the Romans. They worked on farms, but were more likely to be used for housework or for skilled labor in a factory-type workshop. Some of the educated slaves held responsible posts as bank clerks or as tutors. Slaves were even allowed to buy property.

Foreigners living in Athens were another disfranchised group, but many had considerable economic influence.

The worship of common gods and goddesses unified Athens and the whole Greek-speaking world. Each city or region had local deities, but universal homage was paid to Zeus, the supreme god of the heavens, Athena, goddess of wisdom, Apollo, sun god of youth and beauty, and others. All the Greeks respected the prophecies of the oracle at Delphi, Apollo's main shrine. Later Apollo shared Delphi with a newer god imported from the East, Dionysus, god of grapes and wine.

Dionysus was the patron god of drama and, indeed, the world's first great plays were acted out at festivals held in his honor. During his festival held in Athens each spring, the amphitheater was filled with an enthusiastic audience of men and women watching tragedies and comedies performed in the drama competition. The gods were also honored by contests in poetry, music, dancing, and by games: Athena at the Panathenaea in Athens, Apollo at the Pythian Games in Delphi, and so on. The oldest of the inter city festivals, the Olympic Games, was held in honor of Zeus, every four years at Olympia. Even warring city-states suspended hostilities and sent athletes to compete in chariot and foot races, jumping, wrestling, boxing, and throwing the javelin and the discus. (Our modern Olympic Games, dating from 1896, are a revival of the Greek games, but on a truly world-wide scale.)

Many of the Greek gods were adopted by the Romans: Zeus becoming Jupiter, Aphrodite, the goddess of love, becoming Venus, Dionysus becoming Bacchus.

Above: ruins of the great Greek temple, the sanctuary of Apollo at Didyma, near Miletus in Asia Minor. Apollo was the god of music and poetry, light and prophecy and the temple was the seat of an oracle like that at Delphi. Apollo was supposed to speak through his priestesses; what they uttered in a trance was interpreted by priests and decided the fate of men for hundreds of years.

Left: Diana the Huntress, statue from Ephesus, Asia Minor. Twin sister of the god Apollo, Diana was the goddess of hunting, wild animals and the moon. A great temple to Diana (in Greek legend called Artemis) stands at Ephesus, a trading city which lay at the beginning of a route across Asia. The Goths destroyed the temple in A.D. 262.

Right: the Erechtheum on the Acropolis of Athens. This temple was built between 420 and 393 B.C., these caryatids supporting the roof of its south portico. The six statues of young maidens dressed in Ionian tunics are about six feet high. The area between the Erechtheum and the Parthenon temple was the heart of the Acropolis where people met on feast days.

Age of Alexander

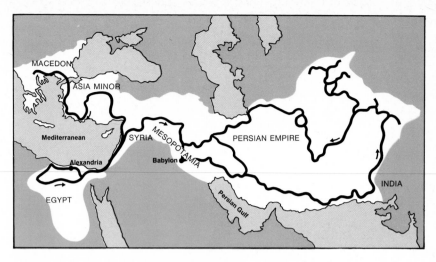

Top: in just 12 years Alexander the Great gathered far-flung lands into a great empire (white). Black lines mark his route, ending in Babylon. Alexander had been tutored by Aristotle, whose ideas gave him goals beyond those of a power-hungry warrior. Opposite page: Alexander, horseman on the left, leads his army against Darius III's Persian forces at the Battle of Issus. As his charioteer tries to drive the royal chariot away, Darius, in the center, looks back anxiously toward the advancing Alexander.

In the fourth century B.C. the Greek city-states continued to make alliances against one another as they had done in the past. They could not make the transition from belief in community independence to allegiance to a larger unit. Meanwhile, to the north, Philip II of Macedon (359–336 B.C.) was planning for the Greeks what they could not do for themselves: to unify them under one leadership.

Philip admired the Greeks, particularly the Athenians, whose civilization was unsurpassed throughout the ancient world. The Greeks, on the other hand, thought the Macedonians were crude barbarians. But the superior culture of the Greeks was no guarantee of success in war and intrigue. In the end the Greeks turned out to be no match for Philip's military skill and tricks of diplomacy. By 338 B.C. he had brought them to heel.

Philip was assassinated two years later. But in spite of this, his Greek dominions remained intact. For when Thebes, Athens, and other Greek cities tried to revolt, Philip's 20-year-old son Alexander proved as able as his father. He lost no time in enforcing Macedonian control. And carrying on where his father had left off, Alexander now hastened to plan the conquest of the Persians.

At a time when the colossal Persian Empire stood astride the Near and Middle East, this was no mean ambition for so young a ruler.

In 334 B.C. Alexander led an army of 32,000 infantry and 5,000 cavalry across the Hellespont (a strait, the modern Dardanelles, separating Europe from Asia). Then he marched down the Asia Minor coast. He dramatically defeated the Persian king, Darius III, at Issus. Then he began swallowing the provinces of the Persian Empire one by one.

In 332 he moved into Egypt, where he founded the city of Alexandria. Continuing east, he added Mesopotamia to his conquests before dealing the final blow to the Persians on their home ground. These rapid successes seemed only to whet his appetite. He crushed the Iranians in Bactria in 329, went on to Afghanistan and at length reached the Indus River.

As sheer exploration, let alone conquest, it was a fantastic achievement. And semi-scientific exploration was indeed one of Alexander's aims. He took with him surveyors, mineralogists and scribes —men who helped him to build up a complete picture of the lands through which he traveled.

Once he reached the Indus, Alexander was just

Greek influence in the East is shown by these coins: 1. head of Alexander on Persian coin; 2. Zeus riding an Indian elephant (Pushkalavati, northwest India, about 130 B.C.); 3. Buddha wearing Greek tunic (Gandhara, northwest India, A.D. 128–150); 4. mythical Greek hero Heracles (Gandhara, A.D. 155–187). Greek culture spread into Asia with the expansion of Alexander's empire.

1

2

3

4

as eager as ever to push on. Now, though, the army's discontent became serious. After eight years of forward movement, wearied by many months of conquering and depressed by the long distance from their homelands, the troops had had enough. Reluctantly, Alexander turned back.

Alexander had envisioned a blending of East and West, encouraging his soldiers to marry foreign women and taking a Persian wife himself. But time was too short for him to consolidate his empire. In 323 B.C. he died of a fever in Babylon.

The history of Alexander's empire now becomes one of disintegration. He left no real heir, so his generals turned on one another, each trying to be his successor. Finally the empire was divided. The three strongest generals established three dynasties: Ptolemy in Egypt; Antigonus in Macedon, with garrisons in mainland Greece; Seleucus in Syria and Mesopotamia.

These three made themselves absolute monarchs, spurning the Greek idea of democracy. Nevertheless Hellenic culture—language, art, philosophy, if not ideals of political freedom—had been brought to a vast area. Trade from the Mediterranean area could now reach China by way of Persia. The Greek mind,

too, was stimulated by Alexander's explorations into unmapped worlds. Advances were made by thinkers like Archimedes and Eratosthenes and by the physician Herophilus (about 300 B.C.). Astronomers theorized about the rotation of the earth around the sun and the effect of the moon on tides.

While Greek thinkers were making these contributions, the East in turn, was influencing the thinking of the Greeks. Kings strengthened their authority by adopting the oriental concept of the god-king. Rootless Greeks, scattered through the Near and Middle East, took comfort in the Eastern belief in life after death. Thus, the way was prepared in these centuries for Christianity, a new Eastern religion that would eventually supplant entirely the old Western gods of the Greeks.

Reconstructed plan of the biggest Hellenistic city, Alexandria, showing the grid street layout and the probable sites of main buildings, including the library which held 700,000 books.

N

Pharos light

Great harbour

Royal harbour

Pharos town

docks

Library

city walls

navigable canal

aqueduct

aqueduct

41

THE ROMAN WORLD

From being a small settlement at a river crossing in central Italy, Rome grew to dominate most of the known world. At one time Roman rule extended from North Africa to Britain, and from the Near East to Europe's Atlantic coast. Western Europe was particularly receptive to Roman ideas of government, Roman civilization, law and language. And even though the magnificent empire eventually collapsed, a rich heritage survived to have lasting influence on the later nation-states of Europe and, through them, on most of the modern Western world.

Roman triumphal arch at Orange, southern France, is one of the largest and most important of those remaining in Europe. Probably built to commemorate the victory of Tiberius over the Gallic chief Sacrovir (A.D. 21), it stands 72 feet high and is 69 feet wide. Such evidence of Roman might can be seen in many parts of Europe and the Mediterranean world.

The Rise of Rome

Indo-Europeans related to those who migrated to Greece in the second millennium B.C. (p. 28) crossed the Alps into Italy sometime during that thousand year span. By about 1000 B.C. farming settlements extended as far south as the island of Sicily, just across from the southwest tip of the Italian peninsula. Such farming tribes as Samnites, Latins, Sabines, Umbrians, Oscans, lived in the plains and in the valleys of the Apennines.

A more civilized people, the Etruscans, arrived about 900 B.C. and settled in western Italy between the Arno and Tiber rivers. Where they came from is something of a mystery. But their recorded customs and surviving relics convince most historians today that they were probably refugees from the chaos in Asia Minor, that followed the collapse of the Hittite Empire.

On the south side of the Tiber, at a ford, Latins chose a site for a small village, Rome. It was dangerously near the Etruscan border but enjoyed certain advantages. The Tiber was navigable to that point, the village was far enough from the sea to be safe from pirates, and its central location was later to aid its growth. For this stockaded hamlet grew indeed —into the chief city of Italy in the third century B.C., and the capital of much of the known world by the first century A.D.

But the character of the Latin people was also a vitally important factor in their incredible rise from peasants to world administrators. They did not flinch from war and seemed eager to put the common good before that of the individual. Their own legends say that Rome was founded in 753 B.C. by a son of Mars, the god of war. This first king, Romulus, killed his twin brother, Remus, baptizing his city in blood at the very outset.

According to the legends, the seventh king of Rome, Tarquin the Proud, antagonized the people

by his despotic use of power. The people deposed him in 509 B.C. and made their city a republic. The two consuls who replaced the king presided over a council of elders (the Senate) and commanded the army. Each balanced the other's power and both were elected annually by an assembly.

Roman expansion began under this republic. The neighboring tribes in the Apennines and the Etruscans were the first to feel pressure from the Romans, losing to them in military encounters in the next century. But in 390 B.C. hordes of blond giants, called Gauls, appeared out of the north, sacked Rome and terrorized the area for months before they withdrew. Periodically the Gauls returned, and the other Latin towns found they needed Rome in their stand against the invaders. Even so, the other Latin towns fought against Roman domination until 338 B.C., when Rome won a decisive victory.

The Romans showed their special talent for consolidating their gains in two ways: by their treatment of the conquered towns and by building a system of roads. Romans went out to defeated cities as military colonists, and some of the people of these cities were brought to live in Rome. The cities were deliberately kept isolated; they could trade only with Rome, not with one another, a policy that increased their dependency on Rome and their identification with her. The roads built to provide fast transport for troops also encouraged union with

Top: third century B.C. ivories of Roman soldiers show typical military equipment: shields, spears, plumed helmets, bronze breastplates and greaves. Originally the Roman army was formed of volunteers, but by the time of Julius Caesar soldiers had become full-time paid professionals.

Part of a banquet scene from an Etruscan tomb painting at Tarquinia, Italy. Sixty painted tombs survive at Tarquinia, most important of the 12 Etrurian cities. These tomb frescoes show that Etruscans hoped for the same kind of entertainments in the afterlife that they enjoyed while they were on earth.

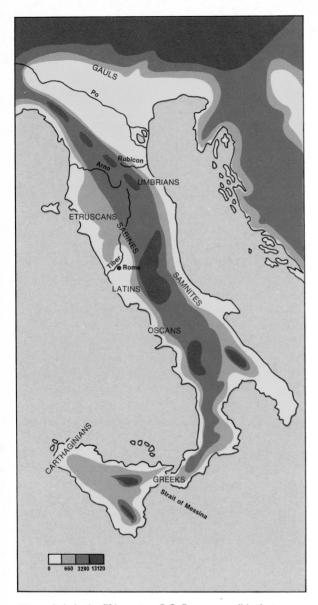

Top: plate decorated with a painting of one of Pyrrhus' war elephants, the first ever seen by the Romans. Two soldiers wearing Greek armor stand in the battle tower.

Above: Italy in the fifth century B.C. Rome, a small Latin town on the Tiber, was to grow into the chief city of Italy by the third century B.C. Other Italian tribes lived in the countryside around Rome. The rest of Italy was controlled by the Gauls, Etruscans, Greeks and Carthaginians.

Rome. The first was the Appian Way, begun in 312 B.C., which linked Rome to Capua. Later it was lengthened to connect southern Italy to the Adriatic coast, making a total of over 360 miles. This proved to be the nucleus of a system of firm-surfaced roads that eventually criss-crossed all Western Europe and much of North Africa.

A combined force of Samnites, Gauls, Lucanians, and Etruscans faced the Roman army in the early third century B.C., vainly hoping to check the city's power. During the course of this war, Rome took Greek colony cities in Lucania in southern Italy. The Greeks at Tarentum (p. 30) sent to Pyrrhus of Epirus on the mainland for help.

In 280 B.C. Pyrrhus crossed the Adriatic from Greece with 25,000 soldiers and 20 elephants. He won two engagements with the Romans (the first at Heraclea, the second at Ausculum). But both times Pyrrhus suffered heavy losses. Then a defeat at Beneventum in 275 B.C. sent him back to Greece for good, and Rome soon headed an Italian confederacy stretching from the Rubicon to the Strait of Messina in the south.

The southern Greek cities retained self-government but also became allies of Rome. At first, people in some Italian cities were given Roman citizenship, in others lesser rights. But, by 87 B.C. Roman citizenship had been extended to all Italians south of the Po River.

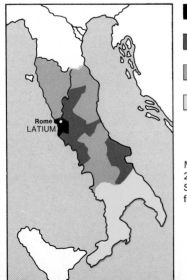

	Roman territory in 500BC
	Territory added by 300BC
	Territory added by 290BC
	Territory added by 275BC

Map left shows stages of Roman expansion. In 290 B.C. the Romans were victorious over the Samnites. Pyrrhus of Greece withdrew his forces in 275 B.C., leaving Rome mistress of Italy.

45

The Punic Wars

Top: the Mediterranean about 270 B.C. The Romans control Italy (yellow), the Carthaginians the western shores and islands (brown), and the Greeks the eastern parts (purple).

Above: Hannibal (left) feared by Rome for 14 years. Right: Scipio Africanus, the Roman general who defeated him at Zama in 202 B.C.

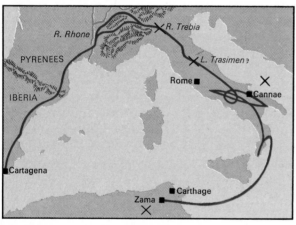

In 275 B.C. Pyrrhus of Greece (p. 45) abandoned his ambition to unify the Greek colonies in the western Mediterranean and withdrew from this area. He had fought the Romans in southern Italy and the Carthaginians in Sicily, and had been defeated by both. After his withdrawal, these two powers were left confronting each other, one in southern Italy, one in Sicily, with only a narrow strait between them.

Other rulers in the east—in Macedon, Asia Minor Syria, Egypt—were also aware of the Roman presence, but the Carthaginians, for years the masters of the western Mediterranean, were particularly sensitive to this upstart power.

In 270 B.C. the Carthaginians controlled most of Sicily, a long stretch of the North African shore on both sides of their city of Carthage, part of Spain, the Balearic Islands, and Corsica and Sardinia. The Carthaginians were descendants of the ancient world's best sailors, the Phoenicians (p. 31) and had a huge, highly-experienced navy.

The long struggle between Carthage and Rome was divided into three wars, called the Punic Wars from the Latin word for "Phoenicians," *Punici*. During the first war (264–241 B.C.), Roman legions drove the Carthaginian army out of Sicily and the raw, hastily-assembled Roman fleet beat back the Carthaginian ships in six out of seven naval battles. Carthage acknowledged defeat in 241, and Rome acquired Sicily as her first province; setting a pattern of government for future conquests.

But Rome and Carthage were still struggling for control of the western Mediterranean. Neither was idle during the years of so-called peace. Rome had taken Corsica and Sardinia by 227 B.C., while Hamilcar Barca was enlarging Carthaginian conquests in Spain. After the Carthaginians violated an agreement with Rome by taking the Greek base of Saguntum in Spain, the Second Punic War broke out in 218 B.C.

Above left: map of Hannibal's route from Spain to Italy and back to Zama. Left and below: Battle of Zama: 1. Initial disposition of forces. 2. Hannibal's elephants charge through breaks in Roman lines while Roman cavalry routs that of Carthage. 3. Romans reform in solid masses, with only Hannibal's reserves left to oppose them and the Roman cavalry attacks from the rear.

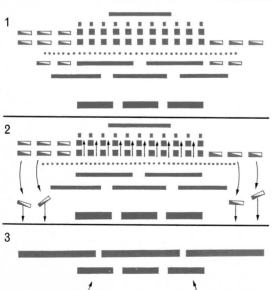

Rome — cavalry · infantry · elephants
Carthage — cavalry · infantry · elephants

Impression of Carthage in the second century B.C. when it was three times the size of Rome and had a population of more than 150,000. Varied styles favored by its foreign architects included Ionic columns enclosing the great round naval harbor.

Carthage entrusted the conduct of this war to a brilliant leader, Hannibal. Like Alexander, Hannibal was young (only 26 in 218 B.C.) and possessed genius as a military strategist and leader of men. A map opposite to this page shows his invasion route through Spain, France, over the Alps, and down into Italy. The Romans were stunned when Hannibal appeared in Italy with about 20,000 men and a few elephants who had survived the stormy crossing over the mountains. This small determined force won three major battles (218–216 B.C.).

Almost all the towns in southern Italy deserted Rome one by one. Hannibal had picked up more soldiers among the Gauls in the north. But he still did not have the resources he needed to take the city of Rome herself. For over 10 years he held his army together, leading it on successful but ultimately inconsequential campaigns, waiting for support from his mother city. Finally Carthage sent his brother, Hasdrubal, with another army over the Alps to join him. When this force was intercepted and Hasdrubal killed in 207, Hannibal knew he could no longer hope for final victory in Italy.

A new Roman proconsul in Spain—Publius Cornelius Scipio—had in the meantime taken over the Carthaginian bases there. Taking a leaf from Hannibal's book, he persuaded Rome to let him invade Africa. Hannibal was forced to leave Italy in order to protect Carthage from Scipio Africanus (as the Roman general was later called). They met at Zama in 202 B.C. Hannibal's army was massacred. Spain and the Balearic islands became Roman provinces, and Carthage was forced to pay tribute.

In the second century B.C. Rome acquired provinces to the east—Macedon and parts of Greece—when she answered Greek requests for aid against Macedonian kings. She was the deciding factor in the Syrian War (192–189 B.C.) against Antiochus III of the Seleucid Empire. As a result of this war, Rome increased her power in Asia but divided the possessions of Antiochus north of the Taurus Mountains and west of the Halys river among her allies instead of annexing them herself.

Carthage was finally destroyed by the Romans in 146 B.C. at the end of the Third Punic War, which had begun in 149. In 133 B.C. the last king of the Hellenistic kingdom of Pergamum in northwestern Asia Minor left his country to Rome as a bequest.

Rome now had undisputed control over much of the Mediterranean.

Republican Rome

Right: mosaic from Pompeii. These gay musicians entertained Pompeians at taverns. Pompeii was a market center for the rich neighboring farmlands producing mainly olive oil and wine.

Statue of a toga-clad member of the Roman senate, most powerful in the third and fourth centuries B.C. The 300 senators chosen by the consuls served a life term of office.

From about 241 B.C. until 146 B.C. republican Rome was gathering fresh conquests abroad. Eventually, this expansion was to be one of the causes of the republic's demise. The army and its leaders became the dominant factor in politics. The greed of the wealthy was stimulated by having new lands to be exploited. The poor grew more discontented.

When Rome set up the republic (p. 44), she gave the king's former authority to two consuls elected annually. The consuls had great, if temporary, powers. The Senate, or council of elders, was the strongest decision-making body, outweighing the assemblies. The government was really an oligarchy, for neither consuls nor Senate were true representatives of all the citizens.

There were two distinct classes of citizens in Latin society: the rich patricians, and the plebeians, with little property and little power. These two classes clashed for centuries over the issue of equal rights.

In the fifth century B.C. things changed in the plebeians' favor. They won the right to have their own officials, ten *tribunes*. In 451 B.C. codification of the laws, the Twelve Tables, gave them more protection from patrician injustice. They even won the right to intermarry with patricians in 445 B.C. By 287 B.C., a law called the *lex Hortensia* had eliminated all legal distinctions between plebeian and patrician.

Nevertheless, the Senate's power continued to grow; even the consuls were subordinate to it. For by this time a clique of wealthy families, both patrician and plebeian, had reserved the magistracies for themselves and, as ex-magistrates, filled the ranks of the Senate. Most of the Senate was made up of wealthy land owners. The experienced ex-consuls and magistrates in the Senate knew all the tricks that could be used to increase their powers and their wealth. They added to their personal estates not only the lands of the conquered but, as the nobles had done in Greece, the lands of poor farmers. Peasants began to desert the countryside, streaming to Rome, or sailing abroad to new lands.

An attempt at reform was made by Tiberius Gracchus in 133 B.C. This tribune managed to get a law passed that limited the amount of public land that one man could hold to 312 acres. The land retrieved from the rich was to be distributed to the poor. The opposition countered this humanitarian act by murdering him. His brother, Caius Gracchus, suffered the same fate when he became tribune and tried to bring about even greater reforms.

From the start the consuls had been in command of the army. It worked the other way around as well, with brilliant generals earning the consulship by their military exploits. For example, the soldier Gaius Marius became consul in 107 B.C. The Senate denied him an army, so he formed one from poor volunteers, waiving the usual property requirement. When this army returned victorious from several campaigns against northern barbarians (Cimbri and Teutones), Gaius Marius further antagonized patricians by measures that gave land to his veterans.

Marius' old foe, Sulla, a military leader with his

own victories in Greece and Asia, finally won a civil war that disrupted Rome between 88 and 82 B.C. and set himself up as dictator. From this point, it was easy for military despots to become emperors.

Marius and Sulla were followed in the first century B.C. by such skillful generals as Pompey (whose campaigns were mainly in the East) and Julius Caesar (who conquered Gaul between 58 and 51 B.C. and invaded Britain in 54). With Crassus, Pompey and Caesar had formed the First Triumvirate, or trio of rulers. In 60 B.C. Pompey and Caesar fought for supremacy after Crassus lost his life in battle in Mesopotamia. Caesar marched on Rome. Pompey fled, and was murdered in Egypt. Caesar became *the* ruler of Rome.

The Romans imitated what they admired—Greek art, literature, architecture. Poets like Catullus and orators like Cicero, both Caesar's contemporaries, could make Latin sing of love or express strong arguments, but both were also influenced by Hellenism. All educated Romans could speak Greek, and the Latin alphabet was based on the Greek one.

Though the Romans did not hesitate to copy when it came to art, in government they displayed a uniquely original flair for dealing with the complex problems that came with the building of an empire.

Top: ornate fountain in the inner courtyard of a Pompeian house. The houses of the wealthy had rooms opening off the courtyard or garden enclosure (peristylium) at the rear. These houses sometimes had hypocausts (under-floor pipes for hot air central heating).

Below left: relief of a butcher hard at work.

Below: a Roman bakery. Grain is ground by donkeys turning huge mills (two lower strips); dough is kneaded and put into the oven (bottom strip); wholesalers buy fresh bread (center strip); bread is carried in baskets (top strip).

Roman Emperors

As the Roman Empire became a world power, enlarged in the first century B.C. by Pompey's eastern conquests and Caesar's victories in Europe, the republican system proved inadequate (p. 48). By 45 B.C. Julius Caesar was as much a dictator as Sulla had been.

Contemporaries described Caesar as a "lover of Alexander." Like Alexander, he won the responsibility for governing enormous areas. And, like Alexander, he did not live long enough to meet this challenge. He initiated agrarian reforms, refounded Carthage and Corinth, and adopted a calendar based on Egyptian astronomers' calculations. But he was still developing other programs when his enemies struck him down in the Senate building on March 15, 44 B.C. (the Ides of March).

In the confusion following Caesar's death, one of his officers, Mark Antony, gained the support of the people; while Octavian, Caesar's grandnephew and heir, attempted to become consul with the Senate's help. Then, in 43 B.C. Antony, Octavian, and Lepidus (governor of Nearer Spain and Transalpine Gaul) formed the Second Triumvirate.

The three worked together for a time, but their decision to cooperate did not survive such provocative acts as Antony's cavalier bestowal of Roman provinces on Cleopatra, the Egyptian queen. War followed, resulting in the deaths of both Antony and Cleopatra. By 27 B.C. Octavian had established himself as *imperator* (commander of all armies). Most Romans welcomed the stability of his autocratic rule after years of civil war. And Octavian announced his intention to "restore the republic" as soon as the emergency conditions permitted. Meanwhile he called himself *princeps*, "chief citizen."

Octavian, now called Augustus, never honored his promise. The Senate still appointed governors for some provinces. but not for those where legions were needed to keep peace. As commander of the armies, Augustus controlled these areas and in reality also controlled the Senate.

With such almost unlimited power he was able to accomplish a great deal. His administrative abil-

Carved reliefs spiral round Trajan's column
showing Roman troops fighting barbarians in Dacia,
beyond the Danube River.

Cameo showing the Emperor Augustus enthroned as a god. Beneath him soldiers drag in newly captured slaves. The first of Rome's emperors, Augustus, brought unity to Rome after a century of civil war, and peace to the empire.

ities were equal to the monumental tasks of reinstating respect for law in a Rome torn for years by civil strife, and organizing provincial governments. He showed wisdom in his decision to set the Rhine and the Danube as the limits of the empire in Europe and the Balkans. When he died in A.D. 14, he left a complicated but workable system to his successors.

To avoid civil war and outbreaks abroad the Senate allowed Augustus' stepson Tiberius (A.D. 14–37) to inherit Augustus' powers, setting the pattern for years to come. Of the Caesars, Tiberius and Claudius (A.D. 41–54) were able leaders; Claudius began the campaign to conquer Britain. Tiberius made government administration more efficient. Caligula (A.D. 37–41) and Nero (A.D. 54–68), however, were both violent and unpredictable.

After the cruel, neglectful, and dangerous rule of Nero (the last of the "Caesar Line") and the assassination of the unpopular Domitian (A.D. 81–96), Rome was ready for what she termed the "good emperors"—emperors not in a hereditary line but chosen for the succession before an emperor died. The second "good emperor" was Trajan (A.D. 98–117), who expanded Rome's limits beyond the Danube and east of the Euphrates.

In A.D. 161 the last of the "good emperors," Marcus Aurelius and Lucius Aurelius Verus, came to the throne as co-emperors with equal powers. When Marcus Aurelius died in 180 during a campaign against Bohemian tribes, at what is now Vienna, he was succeeded by his son Commodus; birth had again become the basis for succession. It was the 12-year reign of Commodus, a licentious spendthrift, that undermined the stability of the empire. After his murder, the legions tried to install their own candidates for emperor.

The 200-year rule of the Caesars and the "good emperors" had been years of relative peace and strong government in spite of palace intrigues and provincial uprisings. Later Romans were to look back to this prosperous time with longing, as the history of the empire became a tangle of intrigue on an international scale.

The center of government and of public life was the Forum Romanum. Here stood the senate house, the hall of records and other public buildings.

The excavations of Pompeii, a city buried under volcanic ash in A.D. 79, give a vivid picture of everyday life in the Roman empire. While the eruption of Mt. Vesuvius rained death on the inhabitants of Pompeii, the smothering ash preserved everything intact, so that even the wall paintings seem fresh.

Pompeii, a port south of Naples, was also a resort where rich Romans relaxed in large, comfortable villas. The basic arrangement of the Greek house was continued in the Roman, which also focussed on an inner court, called the *atrium*. Many of the paintings that decorated the walls illustrated ancient Greek tales. The floors were almost always tiled with colorful mosaics and the walls often covered with scenes in stucco, a technique that

providing great entertainments, as Roman leaders had always done. The Circus Maximus, for example, which according to estimates could seat 250,000 people, was said to have been founded by Tarquin the First (about 616–578 B.C.), but the permanent building came much later.

Perhaps the most pleasing Roman edifice is the Pantheon. This temple of all the gods, constructed about A.D. 125, is roofed by a magnificent hemispherical dome set upon a rotunda. The temple combines the Roman architectural genius for building strong domes with the grace of Greek columns.

Under the emperors Rome became a city of about one million inhabitants, teeming with the business of a people safeguarded by Roman military power. The

Square-sailed merchantmen nearing a lighthouse. Steered by oars, these ships carried grain, oil and wine over the Mediterranean.

required deftness and speed to shape the forms as the plaster set. In the fine houses at Pompeii, mosaics were made from expensive colored pieces of marble in poorer dwellings, from clay tiles.

The streets of Pompeii are straight, intersecting at right angles, with the shops and taverns easily distinguished. There are two theaters; a forum, the center of urban activity, a *basilica* (a hall where business and law were practiced), and two big public baths—the main gathering places for citizens— here as in Rome itself.

The ruins of the Forum, the Colosseum, the Pantheon, and other ancient buildings in Rome complete the picture we get from Pompeii of an organized, constructive society. In the Colosseum, an amphitheater erected in A.D. 80, the public took pleasure in watching life-and-death struggles between gladiator and gladiator, and between man and beast. Emperors added to their prestige by

280 miles of aqueducts carried 8 millions of gallons of water into Rome every day. While the poor and unemployed, who sometimes lived in terrible slums, received free grain from time to time to keep them from organizing a rebellion, and while the old patrician families lived a life of ease as long as they had the emperor's favor, the tradesmen and merchants were busy. Moving goods was safer than ever before. A network of roads ran north and south from Rome and spread through western Europe, linking the cities of the empire to the busy ports. Merchants, with little to fear from pirates on the sea or brigands on land because of the protection of the Roman legions and navy, made fortunes transporting their wares. They took oil, wine, and wool from Italy to Africa and the East, bringing back spices, from Arabia, gold from West Africa, grain from Egypt and North Africa, even silk from China. Money superseded barter as trade enriched the Empire.

Alexandria, Ephesus, Antioch, and Lyon and other provincial cities grew rich because of the easy transport of goods along protected Roman roads and sea routes.

The safety of travel in the Roman Empire made possible the journeys of the messenger of a new religion who carried teachings from western Asia to Rome itself. Without Roman law and roads, it could be that this new spiritual power brought by Paul of Tarsus could not have spread so far.

The Romans liked to decorate their homes with painted murals and sculpture. Scenes from everyday life and mythology were popular subjects. This fine portrait was found in the main room of a house attached to a bakery in Pompeii.

Family life in empire times. Slaves fill goblets and offer them to seated couple. Roman households included not only parents and children but also married sons and their families as well as slaves. Women had no legal status but were free to move about the city and attend public functions.

Latin	Modern	Latin	Modern
Adrianopolis	Edirne	Isca Dumnoniorum	Exeter
Agrigentum	Agrigento	Leptis Magna	Lebda
Alauna	Valognes	Limonum	Poitiers
Alexandria	Alexandria	Lindum	Lincoln
Ancona	Ancona	Londinium	London
Ancyra	Ankara	Lugdunum	Lyon
Antiochia	Antioch	Lutetia	Paris
Apollonia	Pollina	Massilia	Marseille
Apulum	Alba-Iulia	Mediolanum	Milan
Aquae Calidae	Vichy	Mediolanum Santonum	Saintes
Aquae Sulis	Bath	Memphis	*
Aquincum	Budapest	Messana	Messina
Arelate	Arles	Moguntiacum	Mainz
Argentoratum	Strasbourg	Narbo	Narbonne
Ariminum	Rimini	Narona	*
Athenae	Athens	Nemausus	Nîmes
Augusta Treverorum	Trier	Nicomedia	Izmit
Augusta Vindelicorum	Augsburg	Oescus	*
Avaricum	Bourges	Olisipo	Lisbon
Babylon	Babylon	Ostia	Ostia
Bononia	Bologna	Palmyra	Palmyra
Brigantium	Corunna	Pergamum	Bergama
Brundisium	Brindisi	Philippopolis	Plovdiv
Burdigala	Bordeaux	Poetovio	Ptuj
Byzantium	Istanbul	Porolissum	*
Caesaraugusta	Saragossa	Portus Namnetum	Nantes
Caesarea	Cherchel	Rhegium	Reggio
Caesarodunum	Tours	Roma	Rome
Camulodunum	Colchester	Salonae	Solin
Capua	Capua	Sidon	Sidon
Carthago	*	Sinope	Sinop
Carthago Nova	Cartagena	Siscia	Sisak
Colonia Agrippina	Cologne	Sirmium	Mitrovica
Corduba	Cordoba	Smyrna	Izmir
Corinthus	Corinth	Syracusae	Syracuse
Cyrene	Cyrene	Tarentum	Taranto
Damascus	Damascus	Tarraco	Tarragona
Deva	Chester	Thamugadi	Timgad
Divodurum	Metz	Thessalonica	Salonica
Eboracum	York	Toletum	Toledo
Ephesus	Selçuk	Tolosa	Toulouse
Gades	Cadiz	Tomi	Constanta
Genua	Genoa	Turicum	Zürich
Gesoriacum	Boulogne	Verona	Verona
Hispalis	Seville	Vienna	Vienne
Isca	Caerleon	Vindobona	Vienna

Right: map of the Roman Empire during the reign of the Emperor Trajan (A.D. 98–117). It shows the approximate frontiers of the empire, major towns and highways, and also the names of barbaric frontier tribes.
Above: post-Roman names of Roman towns shown on map, the asterisks indicating that no modern equivalents exist.
Below: copy of fourth century A.D. map of Roman roads. Center strip shows Italy with Rome encircled. Though roughly drawn, distances between cities are correctly marked in stadia, Roman units of length measuring about 607 feet.

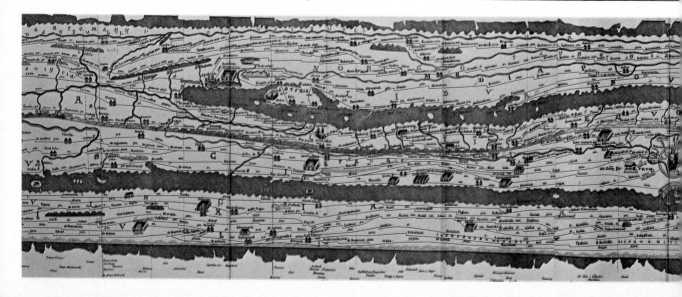

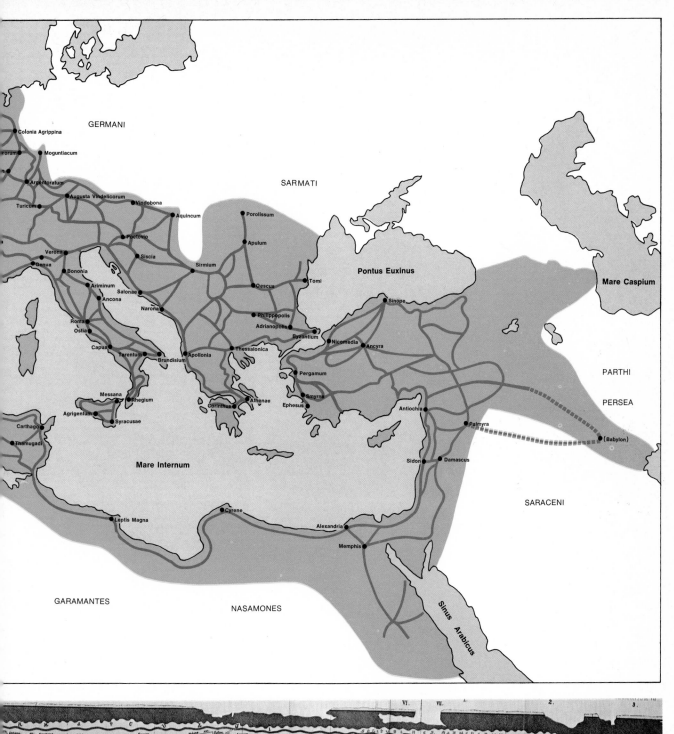

GERMANI

SARMATI

Colonia Agrippina

Moguntiacum

rorum

Argentoratum

Turicum

Augusta Vindelicorum

Vindobona

Aquincum

Poetovio

Porolissum

Apulum

Verona

Genua

Siscia

Bononia

Sirmium

Ariminum

Salonae

Oescus

Tomi

Ancona

Narona

Philippopolis

Roma

Adrianopolis

Ostia

Byzantium

Capua

Thessalonica

Pontus Euxinus

Sinope

Nicomedia

Ancyra

Mare Caspium

Tarentum

Apollonia

Brundisium

Pergamum

Messana

Rhegium

Corinthus

Athenae

Smyrna

Agrigentum

Syracusae

Ephesus

Antiochia

Palmyra

PARTHI

Carthago

Sidon

Damascus

(Babylon)

PERSEA

Thamugadi

Mare Internum

SARACENI

Leptis Magna

Cyrene

Alexandria

Memphis

GARAMANTES

NASAMONES

Sinus Arabicus

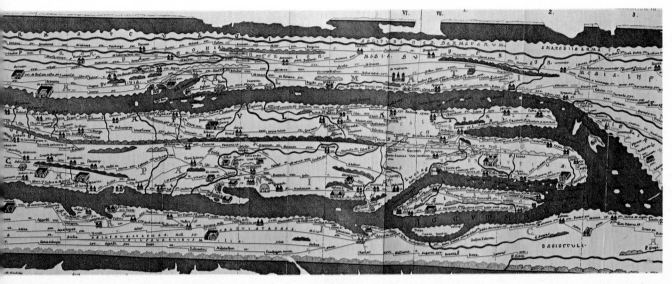

Impressive relics of the once mighty Roman Empire. Above: Pont du Gard, near Nîmes, southeast France. Dating from the first century A.D. this 160-foot-high aqueduct is one of the most spectacular left standing.

Right: theater at Leptis Magna, in Tripolitania, Libya. The theater forms part of the civic center buildings which include a basilica, principal market, and the arches of Tiberius and Trajan. Leptis Magna was a flourishing trade center founded by the Sidonians. It paid tribute to Carthage but pledged allegiance to Rome during the Second Punic War. Its imposing ruins recall its days of great prosperity under the Emperor Septimius Severus (A.D. 193–211).

Judaism to Christianity

Opposite page: map of the Near East shows flight of the Jews through the Sinai desert, division of the Jewish kingdom into Israel and Judah, the Assyrian invasion (722 B.C.) from the north, and Roman province of Palestine.

Top: Assyrian soldier drives Jews into captivity. The Assyrians conquered Israel in the eighth century B.C. Some Jews were deported but the king of Assyria brought new settlers into the country who intermarried with the remaining Israelites.

Below: illuminated manuscript of A.D. 586 illustrates New Testament stories. Upper panel: the crucifixion of Jesus. Lower panel: Jesus rises from the tomb.

Who were these strange people living in an obscure Roman province? Why did they defy their powerful Roman rulers, as they had defied in turn Egyptians, Assyrians, Babylonians and Phoenicians?

The early Hebrews were nomads of the Arabian deserts and were much like other Semitic tribes of that area. Around 1400 B.C. they began to migrate to Canaan, as Palestine was then called, and brought with them their belief in Yahweh, the tribal war god. By 1200 B.C. more Hebrew tribes had entered this land, fleeing from slavery in Egypt. Their leader, Moses, was a powerful religious thinker who introduced the notion of morality to their religion: the god of Moses was a just god who demanded just behavior from his people. He was also a jealous god who demanded undivided loyalty.

Ruled by popular kings such as Saul, David, and Solomon, Palestine was a strong kingdom for many years. But in about 930 B.C. Palestine was torn in two by civic unrest. Israel became the kingdom of the fertile north, Judah the kingdom of the southern deserts. However, the division of the Jewish state did not halt the development of the Jewish religion. Israel chronicled the history of the Hebrew's earlier leaders—Abraham, Isaac, Jacob and Joseph. And in Judah the prophetic tradition of Elijah and Amos was brought to fulfilment by Isaiah and Jeremiah. These writings and the chronicles of the early Jews form the Jewish Bible, or what Christians call the Old Testament.

Further growth of the Jewish religion and the very survival of the Jews as a people were imperiled by the invasions of the Assyrians in 722 B.C. (p. 23) and the Babylonians in 586 B.C. (p. 21). The result was the exile of most of the Jews—by the time of Jesus more than 80 per cent of the two and a half million Jews in the Roman Empire were living outside Palestine—but not the death of Judaism. Throughout this time their belief in the ultimate goodness of God helped sustain them. Their defeats and victories were taken as signs of God's continued interest in those with whom he had made a covenant, or pact, as the "chosen people."

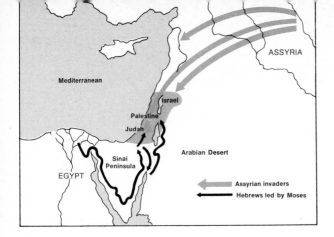

Another concept that helped some Jews in this period was that of the "messiah," or "anointed one," who would free their country from invaders and inaugurate God's kingdom on earth. The belief in the imminence of a messiah was especially prevalent around the time of Christ among various Jewish sects of the Holy Land. (In 1947 Bedouins in Jordan found ancient scrolls in the caves of Qumrân, which were identified as the writings of one of these sects, the Essenes.)

About A.D. 29 in Judea (Latin for "Judah") John the Baptist, cousin of Jesus, announced that a messiah was at hand. Jesus, who was thought by some to be the "anointed one," had spent most of his life as a carpenter in the region of Galilee. But now he went from town to town and spread his new ideas. He did not proclaim a new religion, but like other Jewish teachers he preached adherence to the Jewish scriptures. Jesus had new doctrines however. For example, he urged people to love their enemies and told them that God's kingdom was not of the world but of the mind and heart.

Some of these new doctrines were thought heretical by orthodox Jews and dangerous to the existing order. And so in about the year A.D. 30, Jewish priests of the Sadducee sect arranged to have Jesus executed by the willing Romans.

After Jesus' death his doctrines were spread by twelve Jewish followers called "apostles," or "those sent forth," who recorded the teachings of their leader in four Gospels ("good news"). These teachings formed the basis of the New Testament.

To understanding the origins of what was at first a tiny sect of a small religion we must also take account of the apostle Paul. Though Paul of Tarsus had never met Jesus, his religious ideas, which brought together Greek and Jewish traditions, had lasting importance. Paul believed not only that Jesus was divine and that he came back to life after he died, but that the Christ's (Messiah's) message was for the world, not just for the Jews.

So Christianity was born. Some Jews embraced the new religion and were persecuted for it, as were

Jeremiah, the Hebrew prophet, points to the Messiah who will save the Jews. A halo circles the head of Jesus. Jeremiah foresaw the invasion by Babylonia in 586 B.C. and the captivity of the Jews in Babylon.

those who continued on the paths of the old faith. Jerusalem was destroyed by Titus in A.D. 70 and all Jewish resistance put down, although the heroic defenders of the hilltop fortress of Massada held out until A.D. 73 when those surviving killed themselves rather than fall into Roman hands. A later uprising (Bar Kochba's Revolt) was ruthlessly crushed by Hadrian (A.D. 136). About 580,000 Jews died in the fighting, and more than 1,000 towns and villages were destroyed. The names "Judaea" and "Jerusalem" were abolished, and there were anti-Jewish laws and persecutions. There could have been no greater blows at Jewish national identity. But the Jews retained their religious identity wherever they went (even to the present day), while Judaism's first child Christianity (the second was Mohammedanism) grew into a world religion.

The Holy Family within the walls of Bethlehem. This 12th century German carving on slices of walrus tusks is one of a set of three, probably from an altar frontal or retable.

Christianity Comes to Rome

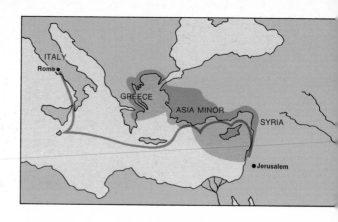

Right: Paul preached in grey colored area; red line indicates Paul's journey to Rome. Opposite page: same region in the fourth century. Dark purple color shows areas of 30 per cent converted; purple, up to 30 per cent.

At the time of Jesus' crucifixion there were only about 120 "Christians." Four hundred years later there were millions. How was this phenomenal growth possible?

During the first 100 years of Christianity, pagan Rome did not distinguish between Jew and Christian. Indeed, at first it was not clear even to the Christians that they were members of a new faith. But the apostle Paul (about A.D. 45–60) let it be known that Christianity welcomed Gentile and Jew alike as he spread the gospel all along the northeastern Mediterranean from Palestine to Rome (where he died). Soon Gentile converts outnumbered Jewish converts.

Within a few years there were Christian places of worship in most of the chief cities of the Empire —Ephesus, Thessalonica, Philippi, Corinth, Athens, and even Rome itself.

Converts quickly swelled the ranks of the new faith. One of Christianity's great attractions was its ready absorption of important features of the old religions. Baptism reminded some of the baptismal practices of Mithraism; the concept of "love thy neighbor" was close to the Stoic precepts of universal brotherhood; Christ's resurrection recalled the Greek god Adonis' death and his return to earth. Christianity also adopted some of the holy days of the pagans. For example, December 25, celebrated as the birthday of Christ, was originally the date of the pagan festival of the winter solstice.

Another attraction was its special appeal to the poor. Christ preached that the humble were especially dear to God and thus many converts were

Left: two 12th century champlevé enamels on copper gilt showing incidents in St. Paul's adventurous travels.
Top: St. Paul disputing with the Greeks and Jews.
Below: friends help St. Paul (in basket) to escape from Damascus.

Opposite page: carvings on Roman sarcophagus dating from about A.D. 350. Christian symbols are combined with those of imperial Rome. Cross in center is surmounted by "XP," first two letters of Greek word for Christ. Wreath around monogram is Roman victory symbol.

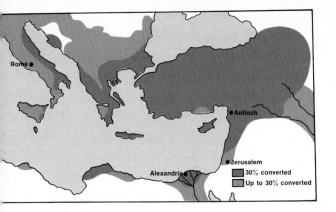

30% converted
Up to 30% converted

Above: miniature of Stephen, the first Christian martyr, from sixth century Greek manuscript. Stephen was stoned to Death for blasphemy by the Jews (including Paul of Tarsus) outside the gates of Jerusalem.

made especially among slaves and poor soldiers.

The first three hundred years of the faith were marked by savage persecution. Although they were tolerant of most of the religions of the Empire, the Romans were angered by the Christians' refusal to worship the emperors and were alarmed at the rapid spread of the faith, especially among soldiers.

The first recorded persecution was in A.D. 64 when Nero had Christians crucified and burned as torches to illuminate a public spectacle. (One of the accusations against the Christians was that they had set fire to Rome. It is possible that Nero was using them as scapegoats, as did later emperors, to divert suspicion from himself.) But the worst persecutions were under Diocletian (A.D. 284–305), when for two years Christians were systematically sought out and killed. However, as was the case with the Jews, persecution strengthened faith.

Finally, in A.D. 311 Emperor Galerius granted Christians freedom to worship as they wished. And in A.D. 335 Constantine proclaimed Christianity the official religion of the Roman Empire.

Constantine's edict reflected the power and wide sway of Christianity in the fourth century. Christians were well established as far east as Persia and India and as far west as the Atlantic Ocean. They were organized as independent local units, which owed respect (but not obedience) to the bishops of Rome. In many of the important developments of the Church—organizing its leadership, establishing the text of the New Testament, wording the Christian statement of belief which prevails till this day, the Nicene Creed of A.D. 325—Rome took the lead.

Beyond the boundaries of the Empire, monasteries and missionaries brought the faith to the heathens. The monastic idea was first established by an Egyptian, Pachomius (about A.D. 290–346), who formed a community of "ones who are alone" on an island in the Nile. Monks built communities as far north as Italy, Gaul and Ireland, where the devout could feel safe from the evils of worldliness.

As the Roman Empire in the West collapsed in the fifth and sixth centuries under wave after wave of barbarians (p. 66–67), the Christian Church, through the strong organization it inherited from the Romans and its secure monasteries, became the repository of Roman and Greek culture.

4

EUROPE'S DARK AGE

Throughout Western Europe, the end of Roman rule seemed to signal the death of civilization. Manufacturing and trade declined. Food supplies dwindled. Law and order came to an end. But a new civilizing force, the Christian Church, was gaining strength. During the Dark Age, until about A.D. 1000, Christian scholars preserved and studied much of the written knowledge of classical times.

Ruins of Roman temple of Venus at Baalbek (in Roman times Heliopolis), in the Lebanon. Built by the Romans, Heliopolis was a large and magnificent city. Here they raised a number of temples between the first and third centuries A.D., including the temple to Helios, the sun god. The Emperor Constantine (A.D. 324–337) is thought to have closed these temples when Christianity became the official religion of the Roman Empire. Heliopolis came under Arab domination in A.D. 637.

Decline of Rome

The vastness of the Empire compelled Rome to maintain large armies to protect the lengthy frontiers—about 6,000 miles from the border in Mesopotamia to northwestern Britain. As central authority in Rome weakened, the provincial armies became political forces.

The legions were often stationed in one area for long periods. Their loyalties were naturally to their commanders rather than to a weak ruler in far away Rome or to the commander of some other Roman army on another frontier. Following Commodus' reign (A.D. 180–192; p. 51), emperor after emperor was deposed by military men who had their own preferences. The provincial armies practically controlled the empire.

Becoming emperor was a risky business. Commodus himself had been murdered. By A.D. 283 at least 15 other emperors had died this way; and most of their reigns had lasted only a few years or less. Others died in battles against opponents for the throne or the enemies of the empire. This constant struggle for leadership seriously weakened the central government.

In spite of political upheaval, during the third century the Roman armies were still involved in border skirmishes; in the provinces they had to contend with such peoples as the Parthians in Mesopotamia, the Celts in Britain, and, as always, the Germanic tribes along the Rhine and the Danube. In the east a new Persian leader defeated Parthian overlords in A.D. 227, and from A.D. 229 Persia was strong enough to challenge Rome in a series of wars.

In Italy, meanwhile, the self-indulgence of the rich and the despair of the poor were expressions of an unhealthy economy. Hard-working peasants had long since given up trying to wrest a living from their own small farms. Landowners left the running

of their estates to slaves while they retired to their villas to enjoy a life of irresponsible leisure. The peninsula had become more and more dependent on the provinces for necessities.

Just as the land was depopulated of people who cared about its productivity, so were the cities depopulated by emigration and war. Trade declined. Civil servants grew ever more unfair in the collection of taxes: Some very wealthy men got away without paying anything at all.

In 284, after a century of short, violent rules, the eastern legions chose an emperor who was able to stay in power for 21 years. This was the army officer Diocletian, an Illyrian born in a village near Salona on the eastern Adriatic. An ordinary man by birth (some say a slave), he had more than ordinary abilities. His efforts to reinstate some order seem misguided in retrospect, but he was the first emperor in a century to dedicate himself to this task.

Diocletian initiated reforms that were to be continued by his successor, Constantine (p. 60). Among other things he strengthened the civil service and separated civil and military authority.

But taxes soared under Diocletian's reorganization, and more and more people left the towns. Markets for luxury goods decreased and severe restrictions on craftsmen, preventing them from changing to other occupations, eliminated any chance for betterment. Diocletian seems to have tried to im-

Above: St. Daniel the Stylite or "pillar dweller" from an early medieval miniature. Christian hermits and monks, isolated from worldly affairs, felt unconcerned about Rome's collapse.

Painting of a baker's stall. With the gradual collapse of the empire many Romans became unemployed or went hungry. To win popularity and gain support, the emperors distributed bread to the hungry masses.

pose stability on the people by force; and some of his actions eventually made it easier for the barbarians waiting in the wings to overcome a populace who had lost all interest in their individual futures as citizens.

All this time Christianity was attracting the growing ranks of the poor (p. 60–61). After Constantine reversed Diocletian's policy of persecuting members of this young religion, and Christianity became the faith of empire, many practical men found it expedient to become monks in order to avoid taxation or military service—at a time when both money and manpower were urgently needed. To this extent monasticism undermined patriotism and Christian beliefs in general tended to lessen the individual's sense of allegiance to the state.

The barbarians in the provinces and on the edges of the empire certainly sensed the growing weakness of Roman resistance. They could see for themselves the decline in such cities as Nemausus (Nîmes) in France, cities that had once impressed them and made them acknowledge Roman superiority.

In the fifth century, the barbarians, lured by Roman riches and driven forward by the pressure of fierce Asian tribes moving into Europe, could no longer be stopped by an overextended, centuries-old system, grown feeble and weak. By A.D. 700 the Roman Empire in the west had been completely overrun by barbarians.

SPQR

Above: often appearing on Roman standards, these letters stand for *senatus populusque Romanus* (the senate and people of Rome). Below: ruins of Palmyra, Syria. Although an important center on the caravan route between the Mediterranean and the Persian Gulf, the city did not come under Roman rule until A.D. 17. Since the people rebelled against the Romans, Palmyra was almost completely destroyed in A.D. 273 by order of the Emperor Aurelian.

The Barbarians Invade

Very early in their history, the Romans had had to contend with the barbarian peoples of Europe. Rome had been overrun by Gauls from the near side of the Alps in 390 B.C. As the Romans expanded north into what is now France and into Britain, they subdued Teutons and Celts. These tribes lived by primitive farming and hunting; only a few of the tribesmen could read or write.

By the fifth century A.D. these provincials had been somewhat romanized—that is, they had become accustomed to Roman law, Roman roads, Roman ways in general. Many of them were hired as soldiers to help defend the European frontier against their wilder cousins to the east.

That frontier had always caused trouble; the Germanic tribes east of the Rhine broke through into Roman territory from time to time. Finally, between A.D. 400 and 500, an avalanche of invasions over the Rhine and the Danube broke up the power of the Western empire.

Almost all of the invaders were Teutonic—Vandals, Franks, Burgundians, Goths, Angles, Jutes, Saxons—speaking an Indo-European language that was an early form of German. But there was another group of barbarians who were not Teutons, and of all the barbarians these most deserved the name in its modern sense.

Theodoric the Great, Ostrogothic ruler who invaded Italy.

The Greek word *barbaros* at first meant only "foreign," or "non-Greek." Ancient Greeks had used the word to describe civilized Egyptians as well as wild men from north of Greece. Much later, the Latin word *barbarus* was extended to mean "soldier," reflecting the fact that barbarians were in the Roman armies. In the fifth century A.D., however, the meaning of "crude" and "uncivilized" could be applied without reservation to the Central Asia barbarians who were now driving westward. These were Huns, a Tartar-Mongolian group, and they were truly a terrible band of uncivilized nomads. Their leader's name, Attila (445–453), was to be used in dark tales in Europe from then on.

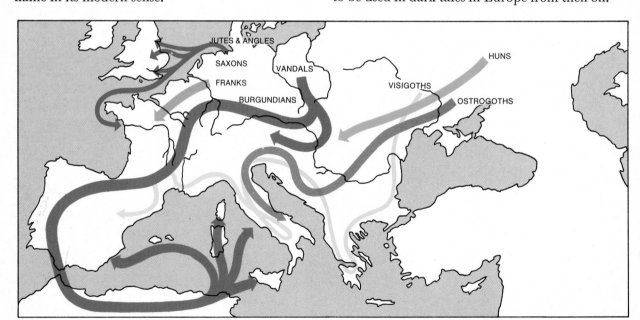

Above: barbarian invasion routes. Fiercest raids came from the Tartar-Mongolian Huns who invaded France and northern Italy A.D. 451–452. Other invaders were the Franks, Ostrogoths, Visigoths, Burgundians partly on Vandals' route, Angles, Jutes and Saxons.
Right: sixth century Europe showing the barbarian kingdoms and peoples. By this time barbarians had sacked and burned the city of Rome twice. In Italy, Ravenna replaced Rome as the seat of government under Ostrogothic rulers.

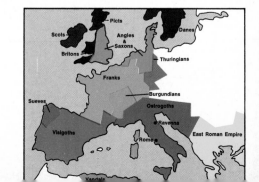

Roman soldiers in armor fight shaggy-haired barbarian hordes (from bas-relief of a third century sarcophagus). Rome constantly struggled against the Germanic and Celtic tribes who harried the northern frontiers of the empire.

The westward surge of the Huns set in motion the movement of the Teutonic tribes. Visigoths (West Goths) and Ostrogoths (East Goths) left the Black Sea area. Angles, Saxons, and Jutes crossed the North Sea to Britain. Teutons crossed the old Augustan frontiers of the Rhine and the Danube, moving into Spain, Italy, North Africa and the Balkans.

The Romans paid barbarians to fight other barbarians—and to fight other Romans, too. For example, when Alaric, chieftain and then king of the Visigoths, first threatened Constantinople, he was bought off with an appointment as governor of the province of Illyricum. Later the Senate in Rome paid him to send his hordes against a usurper who had been proclaimed emperor by the legions in Britain. These attempts to use barbarian strength proved futile in the end. It was Alaric who sacked Rome in 410. (Rome was sacked again in 455 by Vandals.)

Another barbarian king, Theodoric of the Ostrogoths (489–526), was commissioned by the emperor in the East to invade Italy and oust the barbarians already there. The Ostrogoths then ruled Italy from 489 to 554, when the generals Belisarius and Narses reclaimed the peninsula for another Eastern emperor, Justinian (p. 85).

The independent Germanic kingdoms set up by the year 500 in Europe modeled themselves after the Roman system they admired; and their leaders used such Roman titles as "consul" and "patrician." Many married Roman women and some even spoke Latin. In fifth-century Italy, Theodoric retained Romans in his government as officials. One of these, the statesman Cassiodorus, later founded monasteries where copies of ancient Greek manuscripts were made. Boethius (p. 81) was another scholar whose work in Ostrogothic Italy served as a bridge between the glorious past and the uncertain future.

Christianity survived, as well as Roman law and Greek philosophy. The barbarian tribes were converted one by one, then fought one another on the issue of religion. Most of the Germanic tribes became partisans of Arian Christianity (p. 92), while the Franks were allied with Roman popes.

As the authority of the bishop of Rome (the pope) became increasingly acknowledged by Western Europeans, in politics as well as in Church affairs, a new kind of unity was achieved.

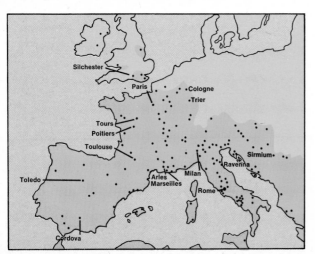

Top: Gregory the Great (A.D. 540–604), a Benedictine monk elected pope, is seen here with the tonsured head of a monk, papal vestments and the Holy Spirit, represented by a dove, on his shoulder. He sent St. Augustine and a group of Benedictine monks on a missionary journey to England.
Right: St. Benedict of Nursia (about A.D. 480–553). He founded the Benedictine order of monks which spread rapidly through western Europe in the seventh century.

Below: limits reached by the Christian church in the early sixth century (orange). Named towns and dots indicate sites where archeologists have found evidence of Christian communities.

The Early Papacy

While the Roman Empire in the West was disintegrating under the pressure of barbarian tribes, the unifying influence of Christianity was steadily increasing. When Rome was sacked in 410 (p. 67), Christianity already dominated religious thought throughout the Mediterranean world and also well beyond it. It was persuasive enough to convince the invaders themselves to desert their old gods and adopt the religion of the empire they destroyed.

How Rome became the center of western Christianity is not clear historically. The apostle Peter, having received his Christ, is traditionally believed to be father of the Church on earth. He is also believed to have been the first bishop of Rome at the time he died (or was martyred perhaps) around A.D. 60. It is St. Peter's authority that has been passed down to each succeeding Roman bishop, or pope.

The designation "pope," from the Greek *pappas* (father), came to mean the earthly father of the Roman Catholic Church. (Similarly, in the Eastern Church the designation "patriarch" derives from *pater*, meaning "father.")

Although in early Christian times the Roman

pope had no special powers in the Church hierarchy, he was endowed with a unique spiritual ascendancy over his fellow bishops because of St. Peter's legacy. In time the pope ruled the territory around Rome.

By the fifth century the papacy had achieved a commanding position in the West, temporal as well as religious, even though the popes held their office under the auspices of the reigning emperors. Later, there were times when popes acted as king-makers.

In the Dark Ages, religious leaders in Europe could not easily communicate with one another or with the people they wished to convert. The old Roman roads, once maintained and patrolled, had fallen into disrepair and travelers were easy prey for marauders. Even so, the Christian word was carried to distant communities by monks who made these hazardous journeys alone or in small groups.

One of the most famous monastic orders is the Benedictine, founded by Benedict in 529 at Monte Cassino in central Italy. Benedict (later canonized) laid down special rules of work and study with emphasis on outdoor labor. The aged and ill copied manuscripts. The abbot controlled the monastery with a stern hand, but the extremes of discipline common in some monasteries were not permitted.

A leading supporter of the Benedictines was Pope Gregory I (A.D. 590–604). Son of a powerful Roman family, Gregory was prefect of Rome for a time. He sold his properties and founded several monasteries, one in his own house. He became a monk but soon was sent to Constantinople where he spent about seven years as *nuncio*, or papal delegate to the court.

Gregory was appointed pope in 590 to the unanimous acclaim of the Senate, the clergy and the public. He strongly objected to accepting the post, but when finally persuaded he attacked his tasks with vigor and intelligence.

This pope earned the name bestowed on him: Gregory the Great. He greatly increased Church revenues and divided them equally among the poor, the clergy, the bishops and Church buildings. He denied the supremacy of the patriarch in Constantinople in Church matters, an enormous contribution to the prestige of the papacy. He also defied Constantinople when he assumed temporal leadership in Italy's struggle against the Lombards, a Germanic tribe who had come down into Italy in 568.

Gregory was very active in encouraging the spread of the faith, sending monks as missionaries through-

Temptation of Christ, illumination from the Book of Kells. This manuscript, including the Four Gospels, was probably the work of scribes at the monastery of Kells, Ireland, in the sixth century. St. Patrick, the patron saint of Ireland, took Christianity to the Irish in A.D. 432.

out Europe and North Africa. Among them was the Augustine who was to become the first Archbishop of Canterbury in England.

After the Romans left Britain, the Britons had reverted to pagan ways under the impact of the Anglo-Saxon invasions. St. Augustine arrived in England in 597 somewhat timidly since he had heard stories of English ferocity all along his journey. Nevertheless he was received cordially by King Ethelbert of Kent, whose wife was already Christian. The king quickly became a convert facilitating Augustine's conversion of others. There were still isolated Christians—some, fine scholars and artists —in Wales, Scotland, and Ireland, but they had lost touch with Rome. The Celtic Christian churches and monasteries were reluctant to accept Roman authority and it was not until 60 years after Augustine's death (604) that Rome fully controlled the English Christian Church.

Top: map of Carolingian Empire showing limits when Charlemagne came to power (dark areas), lands added by Charlemagne's conquests (pale areas) and territory disputed by him and neighboring people (barred). Charlemagne's administrative abilities helped raise living standards in his empire.

Miniature showing St. Mark, probably from an illuminated book designed for Charlemagne between A.D. 781–783. Although he could not write, Charlemagne was a keen patron of culture; philosophy and literature flourished at his court.

The Frankish Empire

In the Dark Age that followed the collapse of the Western Roman Empire, barbarian Germanic tribes occupied most of Europe. They migrated from north to south and from east to west, setting up tribal kingdoms as far south as Spain and North Africa and as far west as the British Isles. In time, all of these pagan tribes were converted to Christianity, which for several centuries was the chief cultural force uniting the people of Western Europe.

By the end of the fifth century, one of the first barbarian kingdoms converted to Christianity had begun an expansion that would eventually make it the successor of the Roman Empire in the West. The Franks, unlike many of the other Germanic tribes, did not expand by moving out of their homelands (western Germany, northern France, and the North Sea lowlands) but added to their original territory, mostly by military conquest. By the early ninth century, the Frankish Empire included most of modern France, Belgium, Netherlands, West Germany, Austria, Switzerland, northern Spain, and Italy as far south as Rome.

Clovis, one of the line of Merovingians (descendants of Merovech, an early Frankish king), was the first Christian king of the Franks. By A.D. 496, the year he became a Christian, he had already united two Frankish tribal groups, the Salians and the Ripuarians, and had added substantial territories to his kingdom by defeating his enemies in battle. After his conversion, he received strong support from the Church for his conquests of the pagan Visigoths and the heretic Burgundians, who were followers of Arianism (p. 92). Eventually, Clovis controlled most of ancient Gaul and part of southwest Germany. He had the old laws of the Salian Franks revised and written down, established his capital at Paris, built there the church of the Holy Apostles (now known as Ste. Genevieve), and laid the foundation of an empire.

However, the empire did not continue to grow immediately. For one hundred years after the death of Clovis A.D. 511, the Frankish lands were divided into two, and sometimes three, kingdoms (Neustria, Austrasia and Burgundy). Occasionally, they were united under one ruler; more often they clashed, in bitter conflict. In the seventh century, although the

Interior of the cathedral at Aachen, Charlemagne's capital, showing the chapel attached to his palace. Charlemagne established many schools including the palace school at Aachen and by encouraging learning helped to increase the number of educated churchmen.

Merovingian kingdoms were again united, they were ruled by a series of ineffectual kings. Power gradually shifted to the royal advisers, the Mayors of the Palace, who were supporters of the Church.

Charles Martel, Mayor, of the Palace from 714 to 741, encouraged the missionary activities of St. Boniface among the pagan Germans and in 732 led a successful attack on a Moslem army near Tours, thus halting the northward advance of the Saracens from Spain (p. 99). Martel's son Pepin, also Mayor of the Palace, deposed the Merovingian king and in 751 was recognized by Pope Zacharias as King of the Franks. Pepin (called Pepin the Short) subsequently supported the papacy against the Lombards and ceded Ravenna and other cities to the pope. This gift, the Donation of Pepin, is considered the beginning of the Papal States.

Pepin's son Charles, who ruled from 768 to 814, was known even during his lifetime as Charlemagne, or Charles the Great, and his name (Carolus in Latin) is applied to the dynasty his father founded (Carolingian). Charlemagne continued Frankish support and protection of the Church forming a close alliance with Pope Leo III. Charlemagne extended his territories by conquest and conversion, adding lands as far east as the Elbe River and the Hungarian Plain. He waged a bitter struggle for more than 30 years before converting the pagan Saxons of nothern Germany. In a dispute with the Lombards of northern Italy, he sided with the pope and eventually assumed the Lombard crown. Although his invasion of Spain to attack the Moors was repulsed in 778, he later established a frontier in northern Spain. On Christmas Day in the year 800, when Pope Leo III crowned him emperor in Rome Charlemagne ruled a territory comparable to the Western Roman Empire.

Brilliant as Charlemagne's reign was, his empire crumbled soon after his death in 814. By the Treaty of Verdun in 843 his grandsons—Louis the German, Lothair and Charles the Bald—divided the already weakened empire three ways. In the century or so that followed, the Carolingian kings were in constant conflict among themselves. The Frankish kingdoms were also subject to new pressures from outside: the fierce attacks of the pagan Vikings.

Sculpture from Charlemagne's shrine shows him dedicating his church to the Virgin Mary. King of the Franks, Charlemagne was crowned "Emperor of the Romans" by Pope Leo III in A.D. 800. He ruled an area comparable to the West Roman Empire.

The Vikings

The last barbarian invasion of Europe gathered momentum in the late eighth century and reached its peak in the ninth and tenth centuries. The invaders from the lands that are now Denmark, Norway, and Sweden, called themselves *Vikings*, "men from the little fiords."

The Viking Age is said to have started in 793, when the Norsemen struck at Lindisfarne, on England's northeast coast. They attacked a convent and a famous monastery and murdered or enslaved the nuns and monks. This was not the first Viking raid, but western Europe was horrified that the pagan and illiterate "Northmen" (or "Norsemen") as the Europeans called the raiders, had made a seat of Christian religion the object of plunder.

The Vikings sought expansion partly because of overpopulation at home. They had tried first to migrate southward but were rebuffed by the Germans. So the Scandinavians looked to the sea. Seafarers by nature and by profession, they were fearless and hardy. They learned to exist in their cold, open boats, soaked to the skin, for days at a time. The Norsemen had developed a craft without equal in Europe—seaworthy, very fast, strong and maneuverable.

The Vikings had no planned political objective in raiding Europe, but their invasions had a decided political effect. Finding they could pillage coastal ports with impunity, the Danes and Norwegians swarmed ashore all over northern Europe. They struck quickly, gathered their booty, and sailed out to sea before the inhabitants could organize to fight them.

The Vikings grew in daring and confidence. Ragnar, a Dane, sailed up the Seine in 845 and sacked and looted Paris and the countryside. The king of France, Charles I, paid him 7000 pounds of silver, and Ragnar sailed home rich. In the winter of 911, a Viking force camped in Normandy. The beleaguered King of France (Charles III) was forced to offer the territory to the Danish leader,

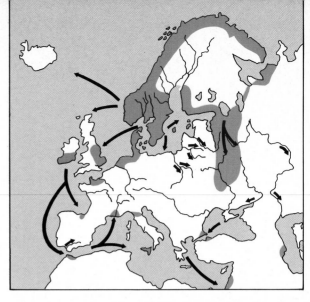

Top: arrows fanning out from Scandinavia show direction of Viking probes by land and sea. Orange areas indicate the homelands of these "Northmen" and regions which they invaded or influenced, stretching from Iceland and Russia south to the Mediterranean.

The Oseberg ship, used for a ninth century Viking burial. In ships like this Norwegian Vikings explored the North Atlantic. Discovering Greenland in A.D. 877, they sailed farther west in the 10th century to become the first Europeans in North America.

Top: embroidered Norse wallhanging dating from the 12th or 13th century. The three figures on the left depict two gods and a goddess. The Vikings eventually adopted Christianity from the Christian people they invaded.

Below: iron helmet sheathed in bronze plates, the property of a seventh century Saxon king. Scandinavian in design, it shows that the Vikings had connections with the Anglo-Saxons across the North Sea over 100 years before Viking raids began on Britain.

Rolf, as a duchy and fief; in return, Rolf vowed to protect the land from further Viking invasion—and promptly filled it with Norsemen.

While Danes and Norwegians sacked the European coasts, Swedes fought, conquered, and traded eastward as far as the Caspian and Black seas and south to Constantinople.

Norwegian Vikings headed westward into the open sea toward Iceland, far out of the sight of land. They discovered Greenland and North America, which they called "Vinland" ("Wineland"). Their settlements in Greenland flourished for 500 years, but the Indians drove them out of America in a scant three years.

As time went on, more and more Vikings settled in the places they raided. The land was more fertile than their own cold, northern countries. Also, the Christian Europeans were organizing to defend themselves, and the Norsemen needed European bases. They chose coastal areas of Ireland, Britain, and France, within easy reach of Scandinavia.

Europe was free of barbarian invaders by the end of the 10th century, but the Viking Age had changed the political face of Europe. The Capetian family held the power once wielded by the Carolingians, who now ruled only a small part of northeast France. The Capetians had won the ascendancy by their successful leadership against the Vikings. England, however, was the country where the effect of the invasions from the North was most marked.

Treasures of a seventh century Saxon king found at Sutton Hoo, Suffolk in England. Top: Purse lid, framed in gold and inset with garnets and glass. The background (now restored) was probably made of bone or ivory. Beneath the lid were found 37 gold coins which enabled archeologists to fix the burial date between A.D. 660 and 650. Right: gold clasp, one of a pair also inset with garnets and glass. The burial chamber which had been made of wood also contained evidence of a ship, 89 feet long. All the ship's timber had vanished; only the impression of her shape remained. In the mid seventh century England was only half Christian and some people worshiped the warrior gods of the old mythology such as Odin, and still performed pagan rites like this burial of personal belongings for the dead king's use in the afterlife.

Below: excavating the barrow (burial mound) at Sutton Hoo in 1939. One of a group of eleven, the barrow revealed no trace of a body but was perhaps a memorial to the dead king. Such finds are important aids to our knowledge of events in Europe's Dark Ages.

Top: early growth of England. Left; shows eighth century Anglo-Saxon kingdoms. Between A.D. 500 and 800 three kingdoms, Mercia, Northumberland and Wessex dominated the island alternately. Minor eastern kingdoms were under the rule of the larger, stronger kingdoms. Right; after the Danish invasion of the northeast, the rest of England united under King Alfred.

Above: King Canute (Cnut) and his wife Aelgifu placing a cross on an altar. Canute, younger brother of the king of Denmark, defeated the Anglo-Saxons in 1017 and became king of England. He combined the qualities of devout Christian and fighting man.

Head of Alfred on penny struck at London. In A.D. 885 Alfred won a great victory there over the Danes.

England's Beginnings

England, as the island kingdom, was always a tempting prize for invaders. Under the conquering Romans, it existed as the province of Britain, a military outpost. But by A.D. 442 the Romans had withdrawn their legions. And in doing so they unintentionally cleared the way for Germanic invaders.

The Angles (a name from which the word "England" was eventually derived), Jutes, and Saxons fought their way grimly into the interior, driving the Celtic population into the western half of the island. As they settled new lands, these Anglo-Saxon invaders imposed their tribal culture and Germanic language on the few enslaved Celts who remained in the east.

In time, a number of contiguous Anglo-Saxon kingdoms stretched in a chain from Bernicia (Northumberland) to Wessex. These were later reduced to form Kent, Northumbria, Mercia, and Wessex. Each warred with the others for superiority. A victorious king, in a first step toward national unity, would gain a temporary overlordship over the other kings. After the arrival of St. Augustine in 597 (p. 169), on a mission to bring England back to the Roman Church, the English Christians also recognized one spiritual leader, the Archbishop of Canterbury.

But the primitive unity which was being created in England was not developed enough to enable its kingdoms to withstand the Danish Vikings who harassed the English coasts in the ninth century. Northumbria, split by civil war, and Mercia, weakened by the loss of Wessex, both fell on the Danes. Wessex, however, under the leadership of King Alfred the Great (A.D. 871–899), stopped the further advance of the Danes. But, though Alfred beat the Danish forces in a decisive battle, he failed to push the Vikings out of England altogether. Instead, Alfred forced them to acknowledge his power in an agreement known as the Treaty of Wedmore (878). Under the terms of this treaty the Danes held the eastern half of England (the Danelaw); Alfred ruled the remainder.

Anglo-Saxon culture reached a high point under Alfred, the greatest of the Anglo-Saxon kings. He set up schools for training future administrators, he spurred on his bishops and priests to write, made poets welcome at his court, even translated some Latin books himself into Anglo-Saxon. More important still, he commissioned the translation from Latin into Anglo-Saxon of the Northumbrian monk, Bede's eighth-century work *Ecclesiastical History of*

Norman ships arriving at Pevensey, southeast England, in 1066 (from the 11th century Bayeux Tapestry). Two hundred and thirty feet long and embroidered in eight colors, this tapestry is at Bayeux in Normandy, northern France.

the English Nation, the first great piece of English historical writing.

English nationalism also took a giant stride forward during Alfred's reign. Even after his death, the overlordship was retained by the West Saxon line of kings, who took for themselves the title *Rex Anglorum* ("King of the English"). Alfred's successors—including his son Edward and his grandson Ethelstan—continued efforts to reconquer the Danelaw; increasing the unity of the country through a common opposition to the Danes.

The newly-won national unity was retained as a result of the statesmanship of the West Saxon kings. They kept Church support through gifts and the encouragement of reform and learning. They avoided rebellions by acting fairly and tactfully toward their new subjects, the Kentishmen, East Anglians and Mercians; as well as toward the Celts of Devon and Cornwall. Furthermore, by handing down the kingdom to their eldest sons, rather than parceling it off among all their children in the Carolingian manner (p. 71), the West Saxon rulers kept the kingdom united.

By the year 1000, England—with one king, one Church, one language—had reached a full nationhood which was soon put to the test. Although the Danelaw had been recaptured by Alfred's successors, the Danes came marauding again in 994 and 1013. Four years later they had conquered all of England and driven the West Saxon kings from the throne. England, along with Denmark and Norway, became part of a northern empire ruled by the Viking Canute (1017–1035).

However, during the entire period of their occupation of England, the Danes had very little effect on Anglo-Saxon culture. The fused culture that resulted was Anglo-Saxon rather than Danish. And when the last of Canute's line died in 1042, Edward the Confessor (a descendant of the West Saxon kings) assumed the throne without dissension.

English nationhood was ready for its greatest test: the conquest by William, duke of Normandy. William invaded Sussex in 1066 and won the throne by killing the Anglo-Saxon king, Harold, in the Battle of Hastings.

Another scene from the Bayeux Tapestry shows the Battle of Hastings where Harold, the last Saxon king of England, was killed.

Holy Roman Empire

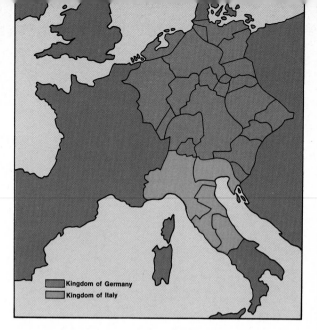

Top: Otto the Great's empire. Its unity depended on harmony between two great kingdoms (Italy and Germany) divided into many semi-independent states ruled by princes.

Kingdom of Germany
Kingdom of Italy

The death of Charlemagne in 814 signaled the gradual decay of his great empire (p. 71) into small principalities ruled by nobility who warred among themselves. The only stable political structure rested on local allegiances based on property. This was "feudalism," a rigid social hierarchy of nobility, clergy, and peasants—either freemen or serfs. The Church itself held enormous properties, so that a bishop often acted like a noble.

With no centralizing authority, ninth-century Europe was vulnerable. German states were threatened not only by Norsemen (p. 72) but also by Slavs and Magyars (Hungarians) from the southeast. (The Slavs and Magyars had been migrating from Asia to eastern Europe since the sixth century A.D.) Norsemen penetrated from the sea up great rivers such as the Seine, the Rhine, and the Elbe. Pressures on the duchies of Bavaria and Saxony, both in southeast Germany, increased as Slavs and Magyars continued their militant immigration.

The impact of these invasions compelled the Germans to consolidate under King Henry I (919–936) of the House of Saxony. In 924 Henry reached a truce with the ferocious Magyars and erected fortifications along the Elbe River. In 933 he defeated them; while his northern armies opened up the mouth of the Elbe, where the Danes had been in control.

Henry's son Otto I (the Great) was crowned king in 936. He resolved to bring the other German duchies under his actual rule rather than rely on the alliances made by his father. The dukes were powerful men with strong armies of their own and it took Otto nearly 15 years to subdue them.

In 951 a lady named Adelaide, who was being forced to marry an Italian prince, appealed to Otto for help. Otto found this a convenient excuse to invade Italy. He made the jilted prince's father (Berengar II) his vassal, crowned himself king of Italy with the iron crown of the Lombards and then returned to Germany to put down a revolt of the dukes of Swabia and Lorraine. The revolt was cut short by the threat of another Magyar invasion. Otto assembled a large German army and decisively defeated the Magyars in 955 at the Battle of Lechfeld, south of Augsburg, Bavaria.

The prestige and power of the papacy were at their lowest during this period. Italy had no cohesive government and Rome was in the hands of greedy nobles who used the papacy for their own ends. Laymen and clergy alike were disgusted with

St. Peter (traditional founder of the papacy), from a mosaic in the Battistero degli Ariani, Ravenna in Italy. By the 10th century the popes had established their authority in Rome, where Pope John crowned Otto emperor of the Holy Roman Empire (A.D. 962).

Otto III, grandson of Otto the Great (A.D. 983–1002). Figures on the left symbolize nations paying homage to the Holy Roman Emperor. Otto spent most of his life in Italy and took little interest in the ruling of Germany.

Rome. Influence was largely held by the bishops, who gave only passing recognition to the pope.

In 961 Otto was called again to Rome to protect Pope John XII against Berengar. In exchange for this service, Pope John crowned Otto emperor, marking the official beginning of the Holy Roman Empire. By the end of Otto's reign, this "empire" comprised Germany and the northern half of Italy.

Otto and the succeeding emperors restored Rome from a state of near anarchy to the stable capital of western Christianity. The papacy was placed under the protection of the emperor and no pope could be chosen without his consent and approval. Roman nobles rebelled, but were swiftly quashed.

Gradually the dignity and power of the papacy was revitalized. At the same time major reforms were being carried out in bishoprics throughout Europe. Meanwhile the emperors continued their struggle to concentrate the power of the local dukes and kings in Germany in their own hands. This was done partly by battles but mostly by undermining the nobles' privileges and rights of inheritance.

The German-papal alliance was the ideal of both popes and emperors. Theoretically, one would handle the religious affairs of the empire, the other would govern. However, a clash of interests was inevitable.

Gregory VII (1073–85), one of the greatest and most popular popes, urged vital reforms that tended to cut off the bishops from some of their richest income. He asserted the pope's right to appoint and depose bishops, to depose emperors, and to forbid appeals from papal decisions. The German bishops appealed to Henry IV, who relied on their revenues to support his power. Together they announced that Gregory was no longer pope. Gregory countered by excommunicating Henry, who then entered Rome in force, installed his own pope, and had himself crowned emperor in 1084. Gregory's Norman allies drove Henry out of Rome, but the savagery of their attack ruined Gregory's standing as the reformer and popular leader of the Church.

Although Gregory died in exile, his valiant attempts to improve Church administration were remembered and the work was carried on.

Coin representing Otto the Great. Crowned king in A.D. 936, it took Otto 15 years to subdue the German duchies and bring them under his rule.

Scholarship and the Church

Religious orders from a 14th century psalter. Left to right: Cistercians, Dominicians, Premonstratensians, Austin friars, Franciscans, Carmelites, Benedictines. Throughout the Dark Ages in Europe, Christian monasteries preserved culture and learning.

In the Dark Ages learning was a rare commodity possessed by few men. The majority of people, the peasants, had almost no opportunity to study even the rudiments of reading and writing. They had to feed themselves and everyone else, and work very hard just to stay alive.

As the feudal system developed under Germanic domination of Europe, each of the three basic social classes performed separate functions: the peasants tilled the soil, the nobility and its armies fought wars and the clergy administered to spiritual needs. Members of the noble families could enter the clergy; but without the special favor of a lord, a peasant stayed on the land, illiterate.

Reading and writing were encouraged by the

Ninth century peasants. Most of these were illiterate; they knew only how to till the soil to produce enough food to eat.

Church, not for the acquisition of learning as such but to keep Christian doctrine alive. The earthly life was transitory; study of the Bible helped the Church to prepare man for the life to come. Limited though the monastery curriculum was, scholarship was pursued with great devotion and discipline. St. Augustine of Hippo (354–430), one of the great early Christian philosophers, found the rigors of monastic student life almost unbearable. Even so, the churches and monasteries were the only places where the literate could exchange ideas.

In later times, more enlightened rulers encouraged education. Charlemagne invited Alcuin of York (735–804), an English churchman and teacher, to supervise his court school and those at several monasteries. Alcuin spent 15 years with Charlemagne, encouraging the study not only of early Church works but of available pagan works as well. In addition to the basic study of theology, he set up a schedule later known as the Seven Liberal Arts, a curriculum closely followed throughout the Middle Ages. (The term "liberal arts" was used in Roman times to distinguish this branch of study—only available to freemen—from the "servile" or mechanical arts.) Alcuin's seven arts were grammar (including prose and poetry), rhetoric (including law), logic, arithmetic, geometry (including the natural sciences), astronomy (with a generous smattering of astrology), and music (mostly the art of singing and the composing of religious chants or plain song).

Alcuin's ideal was pure scholarship, secular as well as religious. Soon other European clergymen were drawn to study other than the Bible. Monks eagerly copied borrowed books to increase the size of their libraries. This borrowing and lending by monasteries was constantly on the increase, to such an extent that some libraries kept exchange catalogues showing the whereabouts of their loaned books and what they themselves had borrowed.

Medieval scholars were well aware of the existence of the Greek classical writers, but their difficulty was in obtaining the original works. They had to make do with the renditions of a few early Christian writers, who themselves had been limited to fragmentary sources.

One of these early writers was Boethius (about 480–524), who translated many of the works of Greek philosophers, especially Aristotle and the mathematicians. In prison for alleged treason, he wrote *Consolations of Philosophy*, read by later scholars as a work on pagan ethical thought. The *Consolations* was translated by Alfred the Great (p. 76) and, 500 years later, by Chaucer.

As learning spread, scholars did not confine themselves to copying and interpreting books. They started writing their own. One of the foremost teachers and writers of this period was Anselm (1033–1109), an abbot in Normandy who later became Archbishop of Canterbury (1093). His monastery, the Benedictine Abbey of Bec, became the chief seat of learning in Europe. Anselm was involved in the Scholasticism controversy: heated debates on the relationship of faith to reason. Anselm and others wrote extensively, attempting to bring the two together into one system of thought. The compatibility of religious belief and scientific reasoning is still a subject of serious inquiry today.

During Anselm's time education was moving out from the cloisters into the streets. Universities were forming. At first they were merely groups of young scholars who gathered in public places to hear such teachers as Peter Abelard (1079–1142). Abelard, who had studied under Anselm, was also a famous French Scholastic. Anselm is sometimes considered the last of the great monastic teachers and Abelard the first great university teacher. Learning had started to live a life of its own, knowledge was now pursued for its own sake in a genuine spirit of scientific inquiry. The so-called "Dark Ages" were a thing of the past.

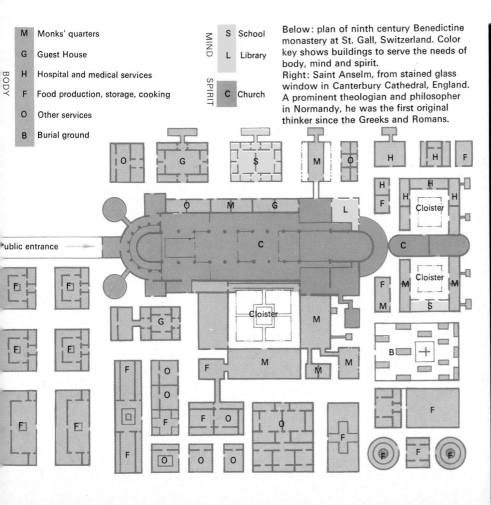

BODY

M	Monks' quarters
G	Guest House
H	Hospital and medical services
F	Food production, storage, cooking
O	Other services
B	Burial ground

MIND

| S | School |
| L | Library |

SPIRIT

| C | Church |

Below: plan of ninth century Benedictine monastery at St. Gall, Switzerland. Color key shows buildings to serve the needs of body, mind and spirit.
Right: Saint Anselm, from stained glass window in Canterbury Cathedral, England. A prominent theologian and philosopher in Normandy, he was the first original thinker since the Greeks and Romans.

Public entrance →

SAINT ANSELM

5
BYZANTIUM AND ISLAM

After the collapse of the Roman Empire much that was Greek and Roman lived on for another 1,000 years in the East Roman, or Byzantine, Empire centered on Constantinople. This rich Christian civilization inevitably came into conflict with another great eastern culture – Islam, which united the Arab peoples and set them, in the name of the Prophet, on the path of conquest.

Rise of the Eastern Empire

By the end of the third century A.D., the government of the Roman Empire had become very inefficient. Bureaucracy, unfair taxation, religious conflicts, and the constant pressure of powerful peoples on the borders had made the empire difficult to govern. But a great deal of the trouble was due to the sheer size of the empire. For it now sprawled across Europe and North Africa from Spain in the west to deep inside Asia in the east.

Diocletian (A.D. 284–305) attempted to remedy this situation by officially dividing the empire into two zones, East and West, with two subdivisions, or "prefectures," in each. One of the prefects during his reign was Constantius, commander of Britain and Gaul. When Constantius died in A.D. 306, his army chose his son Constantine as emperor, following the pattern of a hundred years of such army proclamations.

Constantine attracted supporters to his cause as he marched on Rome. But he met plenty of opposition too. Only after years of campaigning against rival leaders did he establish himself on the imperial throne in 324.

Prior to one of his battles, Constantine is said to have promised the Christian God that he would proclaim Christianity the empire's official religion if he won against his enemies in both East and West.

St. Sophia, Hagia Sophia (Holy Wisdom) or Aya Sofya, the huge patriarchal cathedral built by Justinian in Constantinople (A.D. 532–537) is the finest example of Byzantine architecture. Its great dome, 185 feet high, has a diameter of 107 feet. The minarets were added after it was made a mosque in 1453.

83

Gold medallion of Constantine the Great (about A.D. 274–337). In 306 he became emperor of the West Roman Empire, conquering Licinus, emperor of the East, in 324. Constantine carried out many reforms during his reign, and in 325 called the first Ecumenical Council at Nicaea in Asia Minor. After his death Constantine's empire was divided among his three sons.

Below: Roman world early in the fourth century after the Emperor Diocletian had divided it into two parts. Broken line marks the boundary between Eastern and Western zones. The colored areas are the four prefectures.

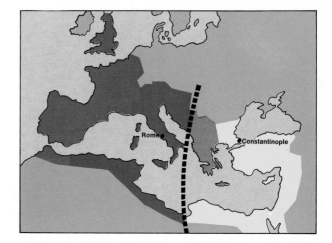

He fulfilled his promise the year after he became emperor.

Aware that his dual empire needed a "Second Rome," he had already selected the old Greek colony town of Byzantium as the site of a new Eastern capital. The completed city, named "Constantinople" in 330, was the first official Christian city in the world. Situated on a peninsula jutting into the strait of the Bosporus, the new city would be easy to defend. Furthermore, its deep sheltered harbor, the Golden Horn, would make the city an important crossroads of maritime trade between Asia and the Western world.

When Constantine died in 337, his capital had greatly increased in size and power, fully deserving to be called "New Rome." It contained a hippodrome—a vast arena for chariot races and other public entertainments—public baths, a senate meeting-place, and many other public buildings, all in the Roman style. A later emperor, Theodosius II (408–450), increased the city's size and built massive triple walls on the land side of the city to protect it against barbarian attacks. The new capital dominated the whole eastern half of the

Map of Constantinople, indicating location of the Hippodrome (center of entertainment) and St. Sophia (patriarchal cathedral). Massive walls (marked by thick black lines) made this the strongest city in Europe. Founded in A.D. 328, Constantinople was capital of the Byzantine Empire until it fell to the Turks in 1453.

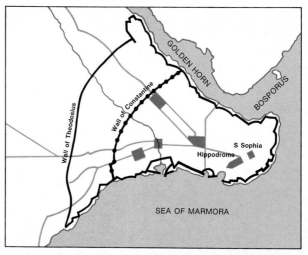

Right: the Emperor Justinian (A.D. 483–565) and his wife Theodora (far right) from mosaics in the church of San Vitale, Ravenna in Italy. Justinian became East Roman Emperor in A.D. 527 and spent many years driving the barbarians out of Italy and North Africa, but his lasting work was the codification of Roman law. His *Corpus Juris Civilis* (Body of Law Civil) became the basis of the law of most West European countries.

Mediterranean, including Greece and its islands, Asia Minor, Syria and Egypt.

Meanwhile, to the west of Constantinople, the West Roman Empire suffered a very different fate. Barbarian invasions during the fifth century harassed and conquered whole sections of the Western empire (p. 66). Visigoths sacked Rome itself in 410 and another group deposed the last Western emperor, then ruling from Ravenna, in 476. Rome, as capital in the West, had lost control of her half of the empire. But the empire in the East continued to expand; and Constantinople's population had risen to nearly a million by the sixth century.

Under the rule of Justinian the Great (527–565) the Eastern Empire entered an age of revival. An accomplished soldier, lawmaker and theologian, Justinian wanted to perpetuate the former greatness of Rome. As Christian emperor he considered it his duty to reconquer the western territories. Led by two generals, Belisarius and Narses, his armies won back the western provinces of Italy, Spain, Sicily and North Africa from the Goths and Vandals, and for a brief time the portions of the great empire were reunited. But in the east the Persians were able to invade Syria, and in the north the Slavs were becoming more threatening.

Perhaps this emperor's greatest accomplishments were the codification of the existing law (Justinian's Code), his attempt to give the entire Roman world a common system of law, and the building of the great church of St. Sophia. This superb edifice was completed in less than five years (A.D. 532–537). Ten thousand workmen were employed in its construction and little thought was given to the enormous cost. When it was finished, St. Sophia, "The Divine Wisdom," was far and away the biggest church in the world. And its rich architectural style served as an inspiration for architects who now designed countless smaller churches in the Byzantine fashion. Many of these have not survived, but St. Sophia still stands in Istanbul (as Constantinople is now called), and its great dome, 107 feet in diameter, still dominates the old section of the city.

After Justinian's death, the West and the East gradually drifted apart, linguistically, culturally and politically. The people of the East became speakers of Greek, not Latin. Eastern thought and culture became more influential.

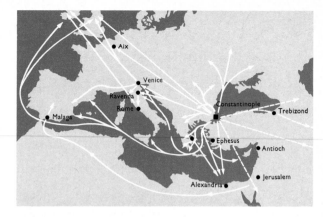

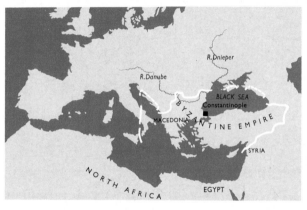

Hunting scene woven in silk by eighth century Syrian or Egyptian craftsmen working in the Byzantine artistic tradition. Court etiquette regulations requiring the use of elaborate figured silks are found in Justinian's *Code*.

Top: map shows Constantinople in the sixth century and the impact of Byzantine culture on the then known world.

Map below: Byzantium under Macedonian emperors with the places named in the text. The empire was smaller than under Justinian and, although the Byzantines still called themselves Romans, Greek was the universal language.

Constantinople's strategic position at the crossroads of trade between the Asian and the Western worlds brought tremendous wealth and power to the Byzantines. The capital city, with its splendid buildings, thriving commerce, and brilliant cultural sophistication was the focal point of a large and imposing empire. It was only natural that Byzantium should become the target for wave after wave of attack from its covetous neighbors, and in the centuries following the death of Justinian the struggle to defend the empire from invaders went on constantly. It was only the adroit use of diplomacy, trade agreements, and the formidable strength of the Byzantine army that enabled the empire to maintain its supremacy until the 11th century.

In the sixth century, the Persians swept through the provinces in the south. At the same time, Avars and Bulgars threatened Constantinople from the north. Emperor Heraclius (610–641) was able to recover the lands taken by the Persians and to hold

off the northern foes. He subdivided the eastern part of the empire into "themes," or military districts, each under the control of a general. This system, later applied to the entire empire, was a very effective way of defending the territories most vulnerable to invasion. Then came an attack from the Moslem Arabs, who invaded Syria, Egypt and North Africa. The Moslems also attacked Constantinople many times, finally withdrawing in 677 after a five-year defense by Constantine IV. Leo III finally put a stop to the Arab onslaught in 739 at the battle of Acroinon in western Asia Minor. This victory prevented the Arabs from moving into Eastern Europe.

The period of political intrigue and instability which followed the death of Leo's capable son Constantine V (740–775) ended with the reign of Basil I, who seized the throne in 867. Basil had come to Constantinople a poor young man from Macedonia. He managed to become the close friend of the Emperor Michael III and later his co-emperor.

Emperor Basil II wearing imperial robes, from a medieval miniature. Byzantine officials kneel at his feet. During Basil's reign expansion of the Byzantine Empire reached its height with the seizure of Armenian and Caucasian lands, the check of Arab advances in north Syria and the subjugation of Bulgaria. Basil's ruthlessness in war won him the title "slayer of Bulgarians."

Basil and his successors were dedicated and ruthless, and it was during the reign of this Macedonian dynasty, which lasted until about 1050, that the Byzantine Empire enjoyed its greatest prosperity and reached its greatest extent. Basil's son Leo VI (886–912) modernized Justinian's Code in a collection of laws known as the *Basilica*. This reaffirmed the absolute supremacy of the emperor over both Church and State and attempted to protect the peasants against the greed of landowners, who, if allowed to become too powerful, could threaten the stability of the emperor's rule.

During the 10th century, Crete, which was used as a base by Arab pirates, and Cyprus were captured by the Macedonian emperor Nicephorus Phocas (963–969). Shortly after this victory, Syria and Mesopotamia also fell to Byzantine armies. By 975 the Macedonian emperors had reconquered vast areas of the empire to the south and east and had extended their influence as far north as Kiev, the old capital of Russia on the Dnieper River. Byzantine missionaries had brought Christianity to Russia, opening the way for friendly diplomatic relations, treaties and trade between the growing Russian state and the Byzantine Empire.

Bulgaria, however, by this time an empire in its own right, was becoming actively hostile again. When Basil II (976–1025), the last of the great Macedonian rulers, came to the throne, he inherited a large but turbulent empire. There were continual revolts in Asia Minor, and the Bulgars, having crossed the Danube, were seriously threatening in the north. In 1014 Basil dealt the Bulgars a crushing blow, celebrating his victory by returning 15,000 Bulgarian prisoners after putting out their eyes. Using his powerful armies, Basil also made sure of northern Syria.

After the death of Basil II in 1025, however, the might and influence of the Macedonian rulers declined dramatically. Authority was replaced by indecisiveness in foreign affairs and the empire's rich landlords took over the administration. The Byzantine armies were reduced in size and strength because of their cost. Aware of this weakness, the Seljuk Turks invaded Asia Minor (p. 106) and the Normans overwhelmed the last of the Byzantine outposts in southern Italy. The Golden Age of Byzantium, which many had thought would continue for ever, was in decline.

Page of the Gospels in Glagolitic script. Probably invented by St. Cyril of Thessalonica about A.D. 865, this alphabet was used to take Christianity to the Bulgars and southern Slavs.

Left: the church of Aya Sofya stands on a hill overlooking the Black Sea at Trabzon, Turkey. It was probably built during the early 13th century. Ruled by Alexis Comnenus and his successors, Trabzon became the last stronghold of Byzantium, for it was not captured by the Turks until 1461. Below: within the church is this superb fresco of the marriage of Canaa. Opposite page: this fresco of the Anastasis (Resurrection) is one of many Byzantine masterpieces in the Kariye Camii (church of St. Savior in Chora), Constantinople (Istanbul), which was built in the sixth century.

Top: ivory panel dating from the sixth century shows Aerobindus the "Consul," the highest honor bestowed by the emperor. Roman ranks and sport, and Greek culture lived on in the Byzantine Empire.

Life and Culture in Byzantium

Byzantine Christianity, centered at Constantinople, was interwoven with an oriental love of pageantry and color. Its spiritual leader, the emperor, ruled from surroundings so impressive in their magnificence that there could be no doubt of Byzantium's richness, power and authority. Constantine VII (912–959), who wrote detailed treatises on administrative and court procedures, recorded that foreign representatives to Constantinople were treated to elaborate ceremonies in the emperor's Sacred Palace. On each side of the throne gold lions roared, mechanical birds sang, and, to impress the visitor still further, the throne itself could be raised high above the floor. Sitting on the throne, the emperor remained silent and motionless while his chief minister took charge of the formalities.

Constantinople was the focus of trade for the empire and for regions beyond. Furs and timbers came from the north, silk and spices from the Orient, and every exchange of goods was taxed. The state, through guilds, controlled the prices and quality of imports and manufactures. The guilds had the monopoly of individual trades or industries; their membership and places of business were under close surveillance by the government.

To maintain the empire, the Byzantines preferred the use of diplomacy, money, religion and pomp to that of military force. A strong, well-trained army was essential, however, to protect the Byzantine way of life. The morals and stability of the army were maintained by the "theme" system (p. 86), under which professional soldiers were paid with allotments of land and regular small cash payments. Men in the navy were paid in similar fashion. The fleet played an important part over the centuries in protecting the extensive coasts and strategic islands of the empire.

As in many other societies, the rich lived in palatial town houses or villas in and around the cities, and also held huge estates, while the poor lived in tenements. The country peasants had small farms which supported livestock and produced grain, cotton, herbs, grapes and olives.

Left: fine 11th century mosaic showing a Byzantine artist's impression of Christ. Countless patient hours and innumerable fragments went to build up such masterpieces of art.

11th century Byzantine manuscript representing villagers sowing and reaping their fields. Peasant farmers had to pay heavy taxes to the state, so many renounced their freedom to escape taxation and became serfs to gain employment on large estates.

There is no doubt of the great agricultural productivity of the empire, but there was injustice in the collection of taxes from the farmers, despite efforts of some rulers to be fair. If the emperor needed the political support of a rich landlord, he might be lenient about this tax. The peasant, however, without influence and without cash, had to pay with labor and products from his farm. He often became a serf on an estate to escape his taxes.

Learning was held in great esteem by all classes. Children of the wealthy were educated at church and state schools and at the university of Constantinople. Poorer parents would sell some of their belongings to cover costs. Even slaves were sometimes sent to school by their owners. Thorough knowledge of the Bible and ancient Greek was required, and mathematics, philosophy, astronomy and law were all available.

The court and monasteries were the chief literary centers. Works of poetry, history and theology, as well as books on administration, were written.

Above all, however, Byzantine culture was most clearly expressed in its art. Pictures of a religious nature covered the walls of every church, either in fresco (painting on freshly spread plaster) or in mosaics of brilliant glass or marble. For an especially rich effect, mosaics were backed by gold as in St. Sophia. The depiction of the human form in sculpture, however, was not found in the churches, and even pictures of Christ, the Virgin, or the saints painted on wood *(icons)* became the subject of controversy in the eighth century (p. 92).

Byzantine artisans were known throughout the civilized world for their skill as gold- and silversmiths, and for their colorful fabrics and brocades. In the sixth century, two monks had smuggled silkworms and the technique of silk making out of China.

The Christian tradition pervaded every aspect of Byzantine culture, as their literature, painting and architecture clearly reveal. The Eastern Church was developing, however, in a distinctly different way from the Christianity of Rome.

Ninth century Byzantine warship attacking an enemy ship with Greek fire, an incendiary liquid made to a secret formula, now lost, which may have included naphtha.

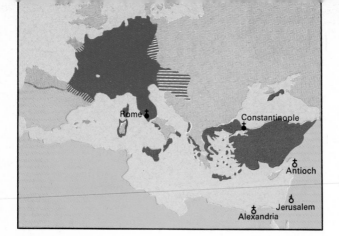

The Eastern Orthodox Church

Map shows the combination of religious and political power in Europe about A.D. 800.
Charlemagne's (Catholic) Empire is shown in blue, the Byzantine (Eastern Orthodox) Empire in red.
The region of Islamic rule with breakaway Orthodox groups is shown in yellow.

As Christianity spread rapidly through the Mediterranean world, almost as many different interpretations of it developed as there were different peoples. Rome and Constantinople had become the chief centers of religion, but the Byzantines, with Constantinople as the first Christian city, felt from the very beginning that their emperor had a superior claim to overall leadership of the Church.

By Constantine's time there had already arisen a fundamental religious question. Were the Father and the Son "consubstantial," that is, of the same substance? The problem came to a head about A.D. 320, when a priest named Arius in Alexandria began teaching the belief that God had created a Son who was divine but neither eternal nor equal with the Father. Arianism had a strong following and the Council of Nicaea was called in 325 to settle the issue. Leading bishops and patriarchs at the Council could not reach agreement by themselves. Constantine, in order to avoid what might rapidly have become civil strife, persuaded the delegates to decide in favor of consubstantiality. The present-day Nicene Creed stems from the decisions of this council.

From this time on, the power of the Eastern throne was an important factor in deciding religious controversy. Councils like that of Nicaea were called to establish the *orthodoxy*, or "correct opinion."

There were five centers of Christian thought: Rome, Constantinople, Antioch, Jerusalem and Alexandria, but when Moslem conquests separated the patriarchs of the last three from the Christians outside Islam, the bishop, or pope, in Rome was accepted as the chief prelate. The Byzantines, however, continued to hold that their emperor embodied the supreme religious authority.

At the Council of Chalcedon (451) doctrinal differences resulted in Egyptian ecclesiasts setting up a separate Christian Church, the Coptic, which still remains in Egypt and Ethiopia. This council also concluded that the patriarch in Constantinople should be supreme in Church affairs, although the forceful Roman pope, Leo the Great, refused to admit of any lessening of his power. The important doctrinal decision made at Chalcedon affirmed that in Christ was true God and true man, divine and human; their union in one person did not destroy their distinction. The Monophysites, who ascribed only one nature to Christ, were declared heretics.

The next great controversy took place in Constantinople in the reign of Emperor Leo III (717–741), who decreed in 726 that images, or *icons*, could not be used as part of Christian worship. To the "iconoclasts," or "image-breakers," they constituted idols and their use in worship was idolatrous.

To the majority of Christians the dispute was serious since they had long revered sacred images. The people in Rome, together with the whole Western Church, were in opposition to Leo's decree. The problem was not settled until 843—after a long period of vacillation—when icons were again permitted. The Islamic and Jewish religions were also against natural representation in art and this fact no doubt strengthened iconoclasm.

The strongest opposition to the iconoclasts came from the monasteries, which were numerous and wealthy. Byzantine monks were widely liked and respected for their asceticism and devotion. It was Theodore of Studium (759–826) who boldly led the monks against the court and publicly proclaimed

Pope Leo IX (1049–54) consecrating a church. In 1054 Patriarch Michael Cerularius disputed Leo's claim to religious authority over Norman-conquered southern Italy. From this time the Catholic and Eastern Orthodox Churches developed separately.

that the emperor's power should be confined to state affairs, that the Church was independent. Theodore was banished, but his fight for the icons was eventually successful. Nevertheless, the emperor retained his supremacy over the Eastern Church.

The iconoclast controversy in the East was a shock to the Christians of the West, just as the installation of Charlemagne as Christian Emperor in 800 (p. 71) seemed an act of treachery to the Byzantines, who believed that the only true Christian Emperor resided at Constantinople. Charlemagne was able to persuade the Eastern Emperor Michael I (811–813) to approve his title of Emperor, but this was done reluctantly and only because Charlemagne ceded control over Venice, Istria and Dalmatia.

The two spheres of Christianity had less and less in common. Among other things, the Eastern Church used the Greek language while the Western used Latin. The final break, or schism, between Rome and Constantinople occurred when Pope Leo IX and the Eastern patriarch, Michael Cerularius, fought bitterly in 1054 over jurisdiction in southern Italy. This dispute arose largely from the personal aims of the two men rather than from any basic religious argument, but it marked the point when the Catholic and Eastern Orthodox Churches in effect turned their backs on each other. The Church of the East would never consent to recognizing the pope as the supreme head of the Church. The Roman Catholic and the Eastern, or Greek, Orthodox Churches from 1054 on developed separately.

Top: Byzantine miniature shows meeting between anti-iconoclastic Patriarch Nicephorus (A.D. 806–815), seated left, and iconoclastic Emperor Leo V, enthroned. Two iconoclasts (center) desecrate a religious image. Nicephorus was deposed by Leo V in A.D. 815 and died in exile. Leo V, who vigorously repressed the image-worshipers, was assassinated in 820.

Emperor Nicephorus III (1078–1081) with St. John Chrysostom, an early patriarch of Constantinople. The Emperor's style of dress shows oriental influence, underlining Byzantium's eastern outlook which helped isolate it from western Europe.

Byzantium Declines

At the end of Basil II's reign in 1025 (p. 87) the Byzantine Empire was at its strongest. Its territory stretched from southern Italy across the Adriatic into the Balkan peninsula and Asia Minor, and embraced the islands of Cyprus and Crete, and part of the Crimea on the northern Black Sea coast. The sophistication, civilization, power and riches of Constantinople were the envy of all the many kingdoms surrounding her. But although the empire was not to fall for 400 more years, the seeds of collapse were already within the capital's walls.

During the Empress Zoë's reign (1028–50) and for 30 years after, jealous nobles undermined the strength of the armies and their leaders, so that the treasury could support their own selfish aims. The

Normans seized southern Italy, ending Byzantine rule there in 1071. The emperor Romanus IV, while attempting to deal with the raids of Seljuk Turks (p. 106) in Asia Minor, was deserted by his generals and captured at the Battle of Manzikert in 1071. The Turks freed him, but his attempt to regain the throne in Constantinople was thwarted by foes at home. From this time on the empire never had truly effective control over inland Asia Minor.

The next notable Byzantine ruler was Alexius I (1081–1118). Alexius had need of his considerable military and administrative talents. Powerful lords and religious leaders had to be won over, and he was faced with Norman attacks in the West. Led by Robert Guiscard, the Normans besieged Durazzo, a Byzantine fortress on the eastern shore of the Adriatic guarding the Roman road leading to Constantinople. Although Alexius bought the assistance of the Venetians, Durazzo was lost and eventually the Venetians themselves dominated the Adriatic. Meanwhile, the Serbs and Bulgarians ravaged the eastern Balkans as far south as Constantinople, where Alexius was able to buy them off.

Byzantium hoped that the First Crusade (1096–1097) would help in the reconquest of the territories

Medallion showing head of Emperor John VIII Palaeologus (about 1370–1408), who spent his last years strengthening the walls of Constantinople for the Turkish onslaught he knew must soon come.

Above: modern Turkish folk dancers on the ramparts of Rumeli Hisar, the castle built in 1452 by Mohammed II to control the Bosporus—a prelude to his siege of nearby Constantinople.

Left: massive triple land-walls of Theodosius II still girdle old Constantinople. Although hopelessly outnumbered, Emperor Constantine XI held these formidable defenses for nearly eight weeks against the Turkish hordes. The city fell on May 29, 1453. Right: portrait of Mohammed II attributed to Bellini shows him in later life. He was 21 when he captured Constantinople.

between the capital and Jerusalem, now held by the Moslems. Alexius persuaded the Crusaders to take territories in the name of the empire and did in fact recover the western coast of Asia Minor after this Crusade.

In the meantime, the Venetians had acquired extensive trading privileges and conducted most of the commerce in the eastern Mediterranean. When Emperor John Comnenus (1118–1143) refused to renew the trade agreements, the Venetians raided in the Aegean until he was compelled to concede. Again, 50 years later, after continual battles with Norman fleets supported by the Venetians, Manuel Comnenus (1143–1180) was forced in 1176 to continue the Venetian privileges and also pay indemnities. The Byzantines were unable to prevent either Norman forays into Greece or Bulgarian devastation in the Balkans.

Then followed the Fourth Crusade. It had been organized as an invasion of Egypt, but suddenly the Crusaders changed course and headed for Constantinople. In 1204 Constantinople fell for the first time—to Western Christians greedy for loot and ready to kill Eastern Christians, strip their churches, and destroy their palaces to get it. The Venetians set up a new empire in Thrace, Macedonia and Greece, and what was left of the Byzantine Empire broke up into small principalities.

In 1261 Michael VIII (1259–1282), from Nicaea, stormed into Constantinople while the Venetian fleet was away and once again the city was under Greek, or Byzantine, rule. Michael founded the Palaeologus Dynasty. This line of emperors lasted almost 200 years but fought a rear guard action to preserve the Byzantine way of life. The empire had lost most of its trade to the Venetians and Genoese, its territories and tax revenues were greatly diminished and its armies were beset on all sides.

Then the Ottoman Turks (p. 107) started pushing through western Asia Minor. They crossed the Dardanelles and, bypassing Constantinople, struck into the Balkans, where they defeated the Serbs at the Battle of Kossovo in 1389, By the early 15th century they held nearly all the Balkans and most of Greece. Both Manuel II (1391–1425) and his successor John VIII begged the Western powers for aid, but to no avail. Constantinople fell to the Turks under Mohammed II in 1453, after a siege lasting several months. The last Byzantine emperor, Constantine XI, was killed in the fighting.

Islam and Mohammed

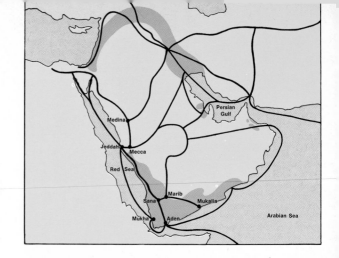

Seventh century Arabia. Chief towns cluster in the more fertile southwest. Arab trade routes cross the desert to Mesopotamia and continue into Asia. Dhows traded across the Indian Ocean.

In the early seventh century A.D., Arabia was a divided land. The northern and central regions were battlefields for the warlike desert tribes. The western and southern coastal fringe (the Yemen) was more settled. Its farmers and traders, living in towns and fertile valleys, had an altogether different way of life, and even spoke a different form of Arabic. Although one empire after another had claimed the territory, none had held effective control. There was little in the peninsula to invite invasion, and the disunited Arabs had offered no threat to their stronger neighbors. Only in the Yemen had there been any stability, where Persians, Abyssinian Christians, and Jewish princes had been the rulers.

The inhabitants of the dust and desert regions were nomads: herdsmen, traders and caravaneers. These Bedouins ("desert dwellers") were led by *sheikhs* chosen from among themselves. The only permanent towns in the desert grew up around the scattered oases. Where these towns lay upon caravan routes, they often developed into fairly prosperous trading centers. Such towns were Mecca, to the north of the Yemen, and Medina, about 200 miles farther north.

In Medina there was a strong Jewish influence. Mecca, however, was a holy city of the desert tribes. From ancient times, Arabs from all parts of the peninsula had made pilgrimages to Mecca to worship at the *Kaaba* ("square building"). This small temple contained a black meteorite, thought by the pagan Arabs to be a deity and the protector of their 300-odd tribal gods.

At this city of Mecca, in A.D. 571, was born Mohammed ("Highly Praised"). An unlettered and improverished shepherd boy, he became in his youth the servant of a merchant's rich widow. When he was 25, he married his employer and became himself a merchant. Of his next 15 years little is known, although he undoubtedly spent much time in thinking out the religious problems that puzzled and disturbed him.

Mohammed regarded the Arab worship of many gods as superstitious and ignorant. Influenced by the Jewish and Christian belief in one God, he became convinced that he had been selected by this God to carry the message of His truth to other Arabs and to the world. Mohammed at the age of 40 began to preach the unity and righteousness of God—at first only among his family and intimates but later in public. He recited verses which he said had been told to him by an angel and which became the basis of the *Koran* (the "recitation"), the universal laws of Allah ("Supreme Being") as revealed to Mohammed.

Thus did Mohammed fashion the new religion, Islam ("submission"), which today is embraced by millions of people. True believers, or Moslems ("accepters"), hold that there is no God but Allah and that Mohammed is His prophet. To attain eternal life, or paradise, a Moslem must make at least one pilgrimage to Mecca (a requirement added

Mohammed ascending to a "Seventh Heaven," from a 16th century miniature. Attended by angels, the prophet is riding Buraq (Lightning), a horse with a woman's face.

Mohammed blessing the Black Stone, which Moslems believe was sent from heaven by God. The Black Stone (probably a meteorite) is now framed in silver and set into a wall of the Kaaba, the chief sanctuary of Islam, at Mecca, Mohammed's birthplace.

later) and fast each day in the month of *Ramadan*. He must be charitable, pray five times each day, and obey the laws set forth in the Koran.

The straightforward tenets of Islam, stressing mercy, brotherhood, justice and eternal life, had great appeal. There were no priests or rituals and none of the complicated interpretations of meaning that so divided the early Christian Church. But many Meccans, fearing they would lose the lucrative business of the Arab pilgrims, opposed Mohammed.

After 10 years of preaching, Mohammed had gathered only a small following in Mecca. The people of Medina, however, invited him to come and establish his religion there. In 622, learning of a plot to assassinate him in Mecca, Mohammed fled that city and made a triumphant entry into Medina, where he was welcomed as both the civil and religious leader. The year 622 became known as the year of the *Hegira* ("flight") and is the first year of the Moslem calendar.

From Medina, Mohammed mounted attacks on Meccan caravans and, in 624, fought and won a pitched battle with a force of Meccans at Badr. The Meccans marched on Medina with 10,000 men in 627, but finding themselves unable to penetrate its defenses, agreed to a treaty giving the Prophet the right to make pilgrimages to Mecca. The treaty was broken by the Meccans the following year, and in 630 Mohammed stormed and made himself master of the city of his birth.

Thereafter, all Arabia acknowledged his suzerainty and accepted the religion of Islam. For the first time, the warring desert tribes and the settled communities of the Yemen were united under a single leader.

The Kaaba (center) in the courtyard of the Great Mosque at Mecca, which every Moslem hopes to visit at least once. When Islamic rule extended beyond the Arabian Peninsula, Mecca, an ancient trading center, retained only its paramount religious importance.

The Arabs Conquer

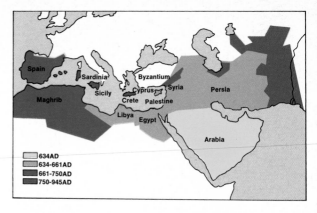

Map showing growth of Islamic Empire between A.D. 634 and 945. 1. By death of Caliph Abu Bakr in 634 2. Under caliphs ruling from 634–661. 3. Under Umayyad caliphs. 4. Under Abbasid caliphs.

In the 11th year of the *Hegira* (A.D. 632), Mohammed fell sick and died. His father-in-law, Abu Bakr (A.D. 632–634), chosen his successor or *caliph*, inherited dominion over his followers, who by then numbered a few thousand. By 657, however, Islam would embrace millions of people of many races.

A faithful follower of the Prophet and a devout believer in the righteousness of Allah, Abu Bakr was determined to convert the whole world to the new faith. First, however, he had to deal with an insurrection. Desert tribes, resentful of taxes imposed for the cause of Islam and believing that with Mohammed's death they owed no further allegiance to a single leader, had rebelled. The new ruler sent troops under an experienced general, Khalid ibn al-Walid, ranging into the desert to quell the revolt. By the end of the following year the entire Arabian peninsula had been won for Islam.

Abu Bakr then set out to carry the new faith to the heathen. But there were reasons for conquest other than the zealous desire to spread Islam. At the end of the civil wars, the Arabs found themselves united and militarily strong. To the north, the prosperous non-Arab towns of the Fertile Crescent promised booty and tribute to the poorer nomads. Raiding and plundering, the Arab horsemen burst out of the desert. The success of these raids demonstrated the impotencé of the seemingly mighty empires of Persia to the northeast and of Byzantium to the north and west.

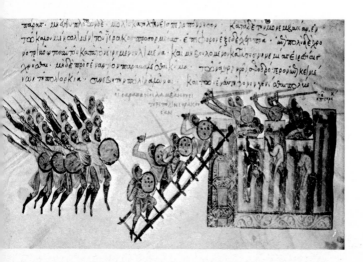

Long years of warfare between the Byzantines and the Persians (the last conflict ended in the year that Abu Bakr became caliph) had exhausted the two empires. Both their peoples had been subjected to ruinous taxation. Persia, torn by dynastic struggles, was particularly weak.

Added to these disruptive influences was a three-way schism in the Christian Church that had split the religious loyalties of Christians under Persian and Byzantine rule. Islam, with its simple beliefs, was like a fresh wind to many of those who had become disenchanted with the complex theological disputes of Christianity. Also, Arab influence was widespread. An Arab prince controlled parts of Persian Syria, and in cities such as Damascus Arab sympathies were strong. To the populace as a whole it mattered little whether they paid tribute to Byzantium and Persia, or Medina—and many were ready to welcome the Arabs as the lesser evil.

The times were ready for the coming of the Arabs, and come they did. In A.D. 634 Khalid drove into Persian territory and raided the village of Hira. Then, making a forced march across the Syrian Desert, Khalid linked up with another Moslem force at Ajnadain, southwest of Jerusalem. Here the Arabs routed a superior Byzantine army.

The brilliant Khalid took Damascus in A.D. 635, but prudently withdrew to the Yarmuk River when two Byzantine armies were sent against him. On the banks of the Yarmuk, Khalid won one of the most decisive battles in history. On a sweltering day in August 636, the Arabs, outnumbered two-to-one, hacked the Byzantine lines to pieces in a series of slashing cavalry attacks. The Moslem forces then swept over Syria.

Impelled by religious ardor and the incentive of booty, the Arabs utilized their knowledge of the desert, the weather, and methods of supply to win victory after victory. Copying their enemies, they flanked each division of their foot soldiers with two wings of cavalry. The swords, shields, slings and arrows of the soldiers were backed up by massive siege machinery—huge catapults and battering

Arabs storming the city of Syracuse, Sicily, which they destroyed in A.D. 878 after a nine months' siege. The Arabs ruled Sicily until 1067, using the island as a base for raids on Italy.

٣٤

وَسَكَنِي وَمُسْكَنِي وَحَوْلِي وَحَالِي وَمَآبِي وَمَالِي وَلَا لَجِئِي غَيْرِ وَلَا

تُسَلِّطُ عَلَى مُغِيرًا وَاجْعَلْ لِي مِنْ لَدُنْكَ سُلْطَانًا نَصِيرًا اللَّهُمَّ اخْرُسْنِي بِعَيْنِكَ وَغُذُكَ

Moslem travelers, illustration from a 13th century manuscript. After their conquests, the Moslems started to develop trade throughout their empire. By A.D. 1000 large camel caravans were regularly crossing Asia and North Africa, and Islamic merchants had established trading centers on the Mediterranean. Great trading towns like Cordoba and Baghdad grew into famous centers of learning.

rams. At sea, too, the swift galleys of the Arabs were victorious. In A.D. 655, off Asia Minor, they destroyed a Byzantine fleet of 500 ships by grappling and boarding.

Aided by their enemies' internal weakness and spiritless defense, the Arabs pushed even farther afield. In 637, though the Arab forces were yet again heavily outnumbered, they won a crushing victory over 20,000 Persians at Qadisiya. Then they stormed the Persian capital, Ctesiphon, and overran Iraq. By 643 all Persia was theirs; and they stood on the very borders of India.

To the west the story was much the same. Here, the Arabs took Egypt from the Byzantines and struck relentlessly across North Africa to the Atlantic. They crossed the Strait of Gibraltar in A.D. 711 and, in an hour's fighting on the Rio Barbate, defeated Roderick, king of the Visigoths, in a battle that was to give them the mastery of most of Spain. From Spain they plunged on into France where they were finally halted by the Franks of Charles Martel at Tours in A.D. 732.

Now the Arabs were faced with the problem of governing this vast empire.

99

Top: Seville cathedral, world's biggest Gothic church, stands on the
site of the Moorish great mosque. Massive brick Giralda tower,
built in the 12th century by Emir Abu Yakub, was the mosque's
minaret. Under the Moors (712–1248) Seville flourished.
Above: ancient Moorish water wheel at La Nora, Murcia. The Moors
taught the Spaniards how to irrigate their land.

Above: peaceful walled gardens of the Generalife (the summer
palace of the Moorish kings) at Granada. After the fall of
Cordoba, Granada was the leading city of Moorish Spain.
Right: the Court of Lions in the Alhambra, Granada, the splendid
fortress-palace of the Moors. With its delicate decoration
the palace is a magnificent example of Islamic architecture.

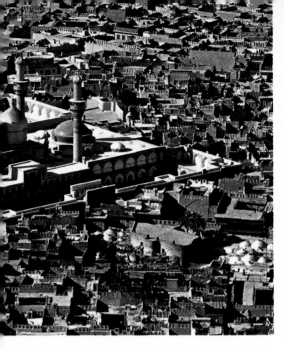

Left: Baghdad today. The tightly packed flat-roofed houses, gleaming mosques and minarets, suggest the Baghdad of the Abbasid caliphs, which was to the west of the present city and which was captured and destroyed in 1258 by Mongol hordes from central Asia.
Right: courtyard of the Great Mosque, Damascus, built in the eighth century when Damascus was the capital of the Umayyad caliphs.

Taking advantage of this unrest, the scheming Abbasid family fomented a rebellion in A.D. 747. Three years later, the Abbasid forces routed the Umayyads in an 11-day battle on the Great Zab River in what is now part of modern Turkey. The new leader of Islam was Abu'l-Abbas (A.D. 750–754), and this first Abbasid caliph inaugurated his reign by massacring all the Umayyad males, and giving important government jobs to non-Arabs.

Wealth and luxury marked the Abbasid years. A magnificent capital was built at Baghdad by al-Mansur (754-755), the second Abbasid caliph. The empire was administered through a complex system of *divans*, which included police, postal service, finance, justice and military affairs. A *vizier*, or minister of state, together with a judge and a

general, ruled the empire for the pleasure-loving caliph.

But the Abbasid caliphate turned out to be no more successful than the regime it supplanted. The expensive and cumbersome Abbasid bureaucracy, coupled with the lavish spending of the caliphs, placed a severe financial burden on the empire. Also, the ruling and wealthy classes had lost touch with the people and with all that was most vigorous in Islam. The whole political framework began to come apart. In the provinces, generals were ruling as viceroys. Given authority to collect taxes, they withheld revenues and, supported by their armies, set up more or less independent domains. By 868 most of North Africa had broken away. By 945 all the territory east of Baghdad was lost as well.

The Moslem world between the eighth and tenth centuries, showing approximate boundaries of regions whose rulers had won independence from the caliph at Baghdad. Although united by Islamic culture and ideas, and tolerant of other religions, Moslems jealously fought one another for political power. Heavy taxes from "unbelievers" subsidized Islamic civilization.

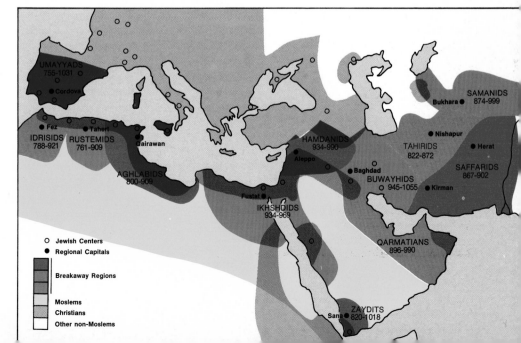

Islamic Culture

Top: 16th century astronomers at a Constantinople observatory. A globe showing Africa and Arabia stands in the foreground. The spread of Moslem knowledge to Europe helped spark off scientific experiment and invention.

Below: physician advising a prince while his assistant prepares a potion (illustration from a 13th century Arabic translation of *Materia Medica* by the Greek Dioscorides).

Although Mohammed was virtually illiterate, he esteemed knowledge, and the caliphs who followed him were patrons of learning. In the next 700 years, several factors combined to make Islam the center of world learning.

Empire-building and the expansion of trade and commerce early provided strong incentives to the development of expertise in mathematics, geography and astronomy. Contact with the sophisticated civilizations under Arab rule stimulated the acquisition and development of a wide variety of arts and sciences. Most important of all, the vast storehouse of ancient and classical learning present in the conquered empire became available to Arab scholars eager for knowledge.

Encouraged by the caliphs, scholars went everywhere, collecting both classical and contemporary manuscripts. The ancient writings of the Greeks, in Persian, Byzantine, and Syrian translations, were put into Arabic. Schools and universities sprang up and flourished in such cities as Cairo, Baghdad and Cordoba. At the House of Wisdom, a center of learning in Baghdad founded by Caliph al-Mamun in the early ninth century, much of the scientific and philosophical heritage of the Greeks was gathered. The mathematics and astronomy of Archimedes, Ptolemy and Euclid, the philosophies of Aristotle and Plato, the medical knowledge of Hippocrates and Galen—all these were collected, translated and studied by Arab scholars.

This borrowing of knowledge reached as far as India, whence the Arabs derived the concept of zero, the so-called "Arabic" numerals, and the decimal system.

Arab cultural achievement, however, extended far beyond their acquisition and preservation of classical learning. They went on to make significant contributions to the arts and sciences.

Mathematicians like al-Khwarizmi (ninth century) and Omar Khayyam (the 12th-century Persian poet) helped to create algebra. Spherical trigonometry was largely an Arab development. Arab scientists carried on objective experiments in chemistry, physics and the science of optics.

For the purpose of making calculations, Arab astronomers built observatories, they determined the orbits of the sun, moon and planets, and developed a number of astronomical instruments, among them the astrolabe, which could be used to calculate latitude in any part of the world. The astrolabe enabled Arab travelers to travel far and wide, making and furthering the study of geography.

Map of the Arab world made by al-Idrisi in 1154. It is drawn with south at the top and for this reason the Indian Ocean appears above the Mediterranean Sea. A Moroccan traveler and map maker to the court of King Roger of Sicily, Idrisi added greatly to the knowledge of the known world.

Hospitals were built throughout the empire—by 1160 there were 60 in Baghdad alone. The chief physician of the Baghdad Hospital, al-Razi (died 925), wrote more than 140 medical works, including a detailed account of Arabic medical knowledge. Another Moslem physician, Avicenna (980–1037), wrote *The Canon*, the most influential medical book in Europe and Asia until the 16th century.

In the field of literature, the life of Mohammed inspired the writing of biographies and histories, while the study of the Koran promoted the study of grammar, philology and lexicography. Arab poets, working in a tradition that went back to pre-Moslem times, wrote lyric and love poetry. Omar Khayyam's famous *Rubáiyat* was composed during this period. Arab travelers recorded their adventures and experiences in foreign lands, and the classic *Arabian Nights* made its first appearance.

Arab buildings, mosques and minarets, original and graceful in design, added a new dimension to architecture. Forbidden by the Koran to depict the human figure, Moslem buildings, furniture and small crafts were adorned with designs from nature and intricate geometric patterns of great beauty.

Skilled craftsmen in metal and leather work, the Arabs also learned to make paper, probably from the Chinese, in the early eighth century. They improved their methods of agriculture by the introduction of irrigation systems, fertilizers and new varieties of plants.

In all respects it was a golden age. Through their preservation of knowledge and through their own achievements, the Arabs profoundly influenced the thought of Western Europe. Crusaders (p. 106), merchants and Christian scholars spread the fruits of Arab culture and scholarship to Spain, Italy, England and Germany.

The decline of Arab civilization was at hand, however, even as the products of its culture were beginning to influence Western Europe. The Arabs, once the conquering barbarians, were themselves to become the victims of a new barbarian invasion.

Islam Attacked

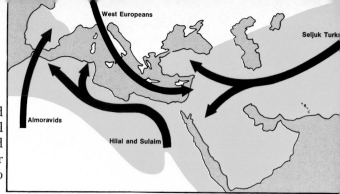

Although by the year 945 the Moslem Empire had virtually ceased to exist, the faith of Islam still exerted a strong hold on the peoples of conquered lands. It even lent its name, its cause, and its vigor to many of the barbarian invaders who were to come later.

By the end of the 10th century, the empire of the caliphs, already seriously weakened from within (p. 103), had lost Asia Minor and Syria to a resurgent Byzantine Empire. At almost the same time, Turks of the Seljuk clan thundered down from the steppe country of Turkestan and swarmed over the remnants of the Moslem Empire. The Seljuks, however, were themselves Moslem converts, and their purpose was not so much to conquer as to restore the Moslem world. Placing the Abbasid caliph at Baghdad under their "protection," the Seljuks recovered Persia, Iraq, Palestine, Egypt, and parts of Syria for Islam and went on to reverse the Byzantine gains in Asia Minor (p. 87). By the end of the 11th century the Seljuk *sultan* ("he with dominion") ruled an empire stretching from Asia Minor to Persia.

While the Seljuks were reinvigorating Islam in the east, other Moslem forces were on the move in North Africa. Sweeping out of Egypt in the mid-11th century, the Hilal and Sulaim tribes ravaged westward to Tunisia, destroying towns and farms.

Map showing internal and external attacks on the Islamic world in the 11th century.

Moslem power in Spain were numbered. By about 1250, determined Christian forces advancing from the north had almost fought the Moslems to a standstill. Their only foothold remained the tiny south Spanish kingdom of Granada. There, though, the Moslems clung on grimly for more than two centuries. Not until 1492 were they finally driven right out of the Spanish peninsula into North Africa.

Christian efforts to retake Spain, however, only foreshadowed the rapidly approaching confrontation between Christendom and Islam—the Crusades ("to take the cross"). The Byzantine emperors, alarmed by the success of the Seljuk Turks in Asia Minor in the late 11th century, appealed to the Latin popes for aid. Pope Urban II (1088–1099) grasped at the chance to extend Roman Christendom and, at the same time, to undermine the power of the Byzantine Church. Urged on by Urban and later popes, Christians from all over Europe—kings,

Left: scene from a 14th-century French manuscript shows a 13th-century crusade with, left, King Louis IX of France landing at Tunis. On the right of the picture a group of saber-waving Moslems besiege French knights. Late 13th-century crusades did nothing to free the city of Jerusalem from Arab rule.

Farther to the west, a sect of Moslem Berbers, the Almoravids ("dwellers in a fortress convent"), seized control of northwest Africa and founded Marrakech (Morocco). The Almoravids crossed to Spain in 1086 and at Zallaka checked a Christian attempt under Alfonso VI of Castile and León to retake the Spanish peninsula. All of Spain south of Toledo passed to the Almoravids.

But there was soon no doubt that the days of

princes, knights, yeomen, pilgrims, even children—answered the call to free Jerusalem from the Saracens, as the Christians called the Moslems. There were other less noble reasons for the Crusades. Freebooters scented plunder; the warlike hoped for glory; merchants wanted to open up the East to trade; criminals saw the chance of escaping justice.

The First Crusade began in 1097. An army of knights and archers, 150,000-strong, marched from

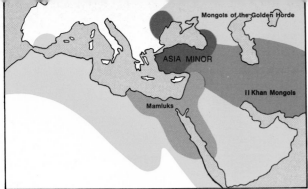

Top: Moslem world at close of 12th century, showing Turkish gains in Asia Minor and location of the Mamluks and Mongols.

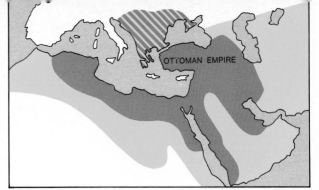

Islam in the early 16th century. Orange shows Ottoman Empire; bars indicate territory disputed by Christians.

Constantinople through Asia Minor into Syria and Palestine to capture Jerusalem (1099) and set up several feudal states. But they failed to keep their early successes.

The Moslems fought back. Under their leader Saladin they recaptured Jerusalem in 1187 and with the capture of Acre in 1291 drove the Christians from their last stronghold.

For the Moslem world, however, the assaults of the Crusaders were much less serious than the calamitous invasion which came from the east in the 13th century. The Mongols (p. 130), hard-riding nomads from Central Asia led by Genghis Khan and his successors, descended on Persia, Iraq and Syria. Halted finally by the Egyptian Mamluks near the Sea of Galilee in 1260, the Mongol tide receded almost as quickly as it had come.

Islam's last great line of empire-builders was now to appear. The Ottoman Turks, so called after their leader, Othman (1259–1326), had supplanted the Seljuk Turks as rulers of a large part of Asia Minor. They crossed into Europe in 1345 and by 1360 had made Adrianople (Edirne) their capital. Before long, Constantinople was virtually surrounded. In 1453 the Turks took the city, under the leadership of their Sultan Mohammed II (1430–1481), known as "the Conqueror" (p. 95).

Left: brightly colored medieval miniature of the Mongol attack on Baghdad in 1258. Inside the city the caliph, on a white horse, rides out to surrender the city to the Mongol leader.
Below: Seljuk Turks in a cavalry charge during a battle in 1048 which won them an east Byzantine province. Before the 12th century the Seljuks had penetrated far into Byzantine Asia Minor.

تقسیم نمودند تمام روز در منزل بابا خرم بخرمی و خوشحالی گذشت واکثر پیشکشهای او پسندیده افتاد

THE ASIAN WORLD

This chapter begins with Persia, an empire which was so prominent in the early history of the Near and Middle East, but which also provided important cultural and economic links with the Far East. There we look at two of the world's most ancient cultures—those of India and China, both more than 3,000 years old. We also look at the ancient civilizations of Japan and southeast Asia, and at the early peoples of Oceania and the Pacific.

Indian miniature in the Persian style shows an exchange of gifts. The prince is receiving his weight in gold. The Persian contribution to painting began at the end of the seventh century when exquisite Koran manuscripts on parchment were common. The art of Persia, where civilizations of East and West met, influenced Asian styles as far away as China.

Persia's Early History

In its greatest days, the Persian Empire stretched from the Mediterranean to the Indus River, and from the Caspian Sea to the Indian Ocean and the Middle Nile. This mighty empire was founded in the sixth century B.C. by Cyrus the Great.

Cyrus was the son of a minor king of the Achaemenid dynasty. When he came to the Persian throne in 559 B.C., he was, like his father, only a vassal lord of the neighboring Medes.

Both the Medes and the Persians were descendants of Indo-European migrants who had entered the Iranian plateau in the second millennium B.C. This larger group, collectively called "Aryans," was related to the Indo-European peoples who migrated to Greece (p. 28).

In the seventh century B.C. Media became a power ranking with Babylonia, Lydia in Asia Minor, and Egypt. Then Cyrus defeated Astyages, king of the Medes, in 550 B.C. and began conquering the rest of the Near East. By the time of his death in 530 B.C., he had triumphed over Lydia, the Greek cities in Asia Minor, and Babylonia.

Cyrus' son Cambyses took the Persians west again, subduing Egypt in 525 B.C. Darius I (521–486 B.C.) and his son Xerxes (486–465 B.C.) had some success in Thrace and Macedonia, but tried in vain to add mainland Greece to the empire (p. 40).

Much of our knowledge of the early Persians comes from the writings of their enemies the Greeks. Yet both Herodotus and Xenophon express admiration for the Persians, especially for the honesty and liberality of Cyrus, and for the administrative abilities of Darius.

From the beginning the Persians were humane conquerors. Not only did Cyrus avoid massacres while winning territory, but after his victories he behaved with great tolerance, allowing his new subjects to worship their own gods and to live

109

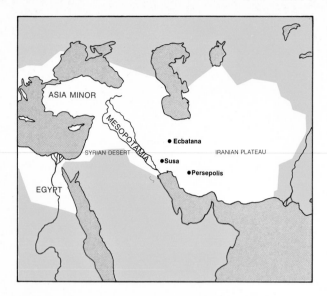

Top: map of the Persian Empire under Darius I (about 521-486 B.C.). Organization of the empire into administrative units is attributed to Darius, who also encouraged trade with other countries and, like other Achaemenid rulers, irrigation of parts of the Syrian Desert and Iranian Plateau.

Left: Persian warrior with spear and combined quiver and bow case (from a frieze at the palace of Darius I). By the fifth century B.C. the Persians had conquered lands stretching from India to Greece.

Khusru Parviz (Chosroes II), last great ruler of Sassanid Persia (A.D. 589–628). Under Khusru Parviz Persian armies battled to within a mile of Constantinople, but before he died Byzantine forces had penetrated deep into Mesopotamia.

according to their own customs. Cyrus gave the Jews in Babylon permission to return to Palestine, a favor for which he is remembered in the Bible.

Darius I governed the empire through *satraps* (provincial governors) and introduced many improvements for the benefit of the people: irrigation, the introduction of coins to facilitate trade, and a highway system serving both economic and military purposes. Inspectors called "king's eyes" used these roads too, checking on the loyalty and efficiency of the satraps. Towns and trade flourished and a system of banking which involved the use of bank checks was inaugurated. Persian explorers sailed as far away as North and West Africa.

The religion adopted by the time of Xerxes reflects Persian intellectual and ethical values. The nature gods Mithras (the sun), Mah (the moon), Atar (fire), and others were discarded by the prophet Zoroaster (Zarathustra) in favor of one god, Ahura Mazda, "wise lord." Hymns in the *Avesta*, the Zoroastrian Bible, emphasize the desire for wisdom so that good can be preferred to evil.

In 331–332 B.C. the Macedonian conqueror Alexander crushed the Persian Empire and burned the capital Persepolis. His Greek successors, the Seleucids (p. 41) however, were not able to hold all the Eastern lands. In 249 B.C. a Parthian kingdom

Top: fourth century sardonyx cameo commemorating the defeat of the Roman army by the Persians and the capture of the Roman Emperor Valerian in A.D. 260. He remained the prisoner of Shapur I, the ruler of Sassanid Persia, for the rest of his life.

Below: seventh century B.C. Persian rhyton (drinking horn).

was established southeast of the Caspian Sea. By the first century A.D., it was an Eastern empire, with Persia one of its dominions.

The Persian king Ardashir I, a vassal of the Parthians as Cyrus had been of the Medes, defeated the Parthians and made Persia an Eastern power again in 226 A.D. From this time on, for four centuries, Persians of the Sassanid dynasty were active foes of the Roman Empire and Byzantium.

Under the leadership of the Sassanians, Persia became a strong military and political power, and making the most of its position between East and West, grew rich through trade. Roman silver and Chinese silk, Greek medical knowledge and Indian astronomy met and crossed in Persia.

A new religion made its appearance about A.D. 215–273, when a Persian nobleman named Mani began preaching a blend of elements from Zoroastrianism, Buddhism, and Christianity. Manichaeism, as it was called, attempted, by reconciling religious differences, to provide a new state religion. The attempt failed, but Manichaeism, spread as far as North Africa, China and Europe.

The splendid Persian Empire of the Sassanids was weakened over a span of 400 years by repeated wars. In A.D. 641 the Arabs conquered Persia, which they treated as a favored province.

Aryan India

In the second millennium B.C. fair-skinned Indo-Europeans crossed the Hindu Kush mountains into India. They called themselves Aryans, or "nobles." (The Persians were also of this branch; "Iran" derives from an Old Persian word very similar to "Aryan.") As they moved South, the Aryans crushed the Indus Valley civilization of the Dravidians, a short, dark-skinned people who tended to become the serfs or slaves of their conquerors.

Our main source for the history of this early period is the *Rig-Veda*, ancient hymns recorded around 1000 B.C. Allusions are made to battles for pastureland against the indigenous people and between Aryan tribes. The chief of a tribe, or *raja*, was mainly a war leader, sharing power with the priests and with tribal councils.

The Aryan tribes had settled mainly in the fertile northern plains of the Indus and Ganges river valleys. There they herded cattle, goats, and sheep, grew grain, and made tools and weapons of bronze. But they did not build cities for a long time.

Although early Aryan life was still tribal, there were already different classes: nobles and warriors *(kshatriyas)*, priests *(brahmans)*, peasants and artisans *(vaishyas)*. A fourth class of serfs *(shudras)* was added as Aryans became masters of the Dravidians.

Through the centuries there was some shift in the make-up of these classes, or castes, but the lines between them became harder to cross. An Aryan could move down in the scale quickly enough, or become an outcast by marrying a non-Aryan, but moving up was a different matter. The Brahmans wove the caste system into religion, thus protecting their own high status, which they further reinforced by making the ritual more and more complex.

Most of the gods of Brahmanism—Indra (god of the air and rain), Agni (god of fire), Dyaus (god of the sky), and so on—were old Vedic gods that resembled those of the Greeks and Romans. Mitra, a sun god, is found in the early Persian pantheon as Mithras.

Between about 800 B.C. and 500 B.C., the Aryans expanded eastward along the Ganges river. One ancient poem, the *Mahabharata*, dramatizes as a great war what was probably a tribal clash, but neither the time nor the participants can be pinpointed. Sacred writings, however, provide specific information about religious doctrines. The *Upanishads* ("confidential teachings"), for example, recorded sometime between 600 and 300 B.C., introduced the idea of the endless rebirth of man *(sam-*

Paying homage to Buddha, from a 2000-year old relief. Upper panel shows the gods adoring a relic of the Buddha and lower panel depicts worship of an enthroned but invisible Buddha. Before Greek influence reached India, Buddha was never portrayed by Indian artists because he was regarded as superhuman.

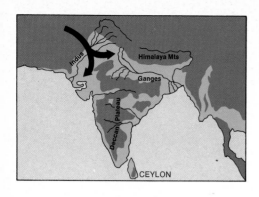

Left: map of India and Ceylon showing highland regions (dark areas), lowlands and principal rivers. Arrows indicate the routes of Aryan invaders into northwest India.

Right: Agni, Aryan god of fire. Hindu artists often picture him with two faces to show the opposing aspects of his character, both beneficial and destructive.

sara), his station in each life determined by his actions in former lives *(karma)*. This idea helped the priests maintain the caste system.

As Brahmanism grew stronger, dissenters inevitably challenged it. The Jains (sixth century B.C.) preached asceticism. They sought physical pain and isolated themselves in forests.

Another alternative to Brahmanism was supplied by Siddhartha Gautama, a northern prince who was born about 560 B.C. Siddhartha gave up his princely life to seek the reason for human misery. After years of wandering, the truth was revealed to him. His revelation joined the old idea of *karma* with *Nirvana*, a final release from having to undergo sorrow in life after life. The individual self could achieve *Nirvana* (union with the Self of the universe) by a life of meditation, moderation and altruism.

Siddhartha's teachings earned him the title of Buddha, "Enlightened One." By the third century B.C. Buddhism had many monasteries and temples all over India, co-existing with Brahmanism, Jainism, and other religions.

Meanwhile, incursions from the West—Darius of Persia in the sixth century, Alexander of Macedonia in the fourth—had reached the Indus River. India seems to have learned something about empire from these western rulers, however. Only four years or so after Alexander turned back in 325 B.C., an Indian leader began to unify the small kingdoms of Northern India.

First century sculpture of Siddhartha beginning the journey on which he received enlightenment and became Buddha. He and his first disciples founded an order of monks who spread his teachings throughout India. When Buddha died about 483 B.C. his ashes were distributed in burial mounds.

The Mauryan Empire

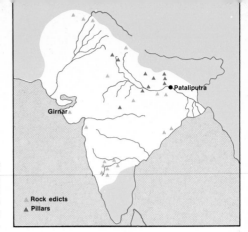

Mauryan Empire (white) during the reign of Asoka, its most famous ruler. Map shows Pataliputra, the capital (modern Patna), and indicates the location of rock edicts and large inscribed stone pillars erected by Asoka to publicize Buddhist ideals.

Chandragupta Maurya (about 321–297 B.C.), India's first empire-builder, was not born to the ruling class but was a member of a low caste, probably the *vaishya*. He was fortunate in having an able adviser, the Brahman Kautalya, and also had the wit to recognize wise advice and the vigor to act on it. When he came to power, India was divided among many small kingdoms, Aryan in the north and Dravidian in the south.

In the first part of his reign, Chandragupta overpowered the petty states of Northern India, many of them already disorganized by Alexander's progress. The Greek garrisons Alexander left behind could not halt his advance. Nor could Nicator, the Seleucid king. Chandragupta defeated Nicator in 303 B.C. but gave the latter 500 elephants to console him for the loss of parts of Afghanistan.

These former enemies apparently learned mutual respect on the battlefield and at the conference table, for from that time Chandragupta's court at Pataliputra was a meeting place for Greek and Indian. One of the Greek envoys, Megasthenes, wrote about his life at the Indian court and his travels in the emerging Indian state. He approved of the orderly and sophisticated administrative system which Chandragupta instituted.

Chandragupta's advisers and a secret service kept surveillance on the local administrations in the conquered kingdoms. The king exercised economic control over his subjects by using the existing methods of tax collection. The Indians had begun using coined money, but taxes were also collected in the form of rice, goats and precious stones. The records of payment were inscribed in Sanskrit, Pali, or one of the other Indian scripts on stone or metal tablets.

The Hindu god Ganesha, a painted sculpture from the Royal Palace of Nepal. The elephant-headed son of Siva and Parvati, Ganesha is the bringer of good luck and god of prudence. Hindus also believe that the goddess Parvati influences everyday affairs.

Above: Great Stupa, Sanchi in central India. This shrine, one of the oldest surviving Buddhist structures in the world, was built during Asoka's reign. The shape of stupas symbolizes the cosmos, the dome representing heaven, and a central shaft the axis of the earth. Many stupas were built in memory of Buddha.

Chandragupta did what the Persians had done before him: he built a system of roads to speed up communications and constructed dams, wells and irrigation projects to show his concern for the farmer. Traders and merchants also benefited from Chandragupta's stable government and improved roads.

Under the reign of Chandragupta's grandson, Asoka (about 274–236 B.C.), the Mauryan Empire attained its greatest power and brilliance. Asoka added nearly all of the subcontinent of India to the Mauryan Empire. Only the southern tip remained independent. After the struggle to take Kalinga in the southeast (about 260 B.C.), when hundreds of thousands were killed or taken prisoner, Asoka rejected war. He had his Buddhist precepts carved on rocks and stone pillars throughout India, using local languages. He spread a new moral concept called *dharma*, a flexible word encompassing piety, honesty, tolerance, respect for elders and for all life. "All men are my children," said Asoka, and he meant men in Burma and Ceylon, in Syria, Egypt and Macedonia, as well as in India. Buddhist missionaries were sent to all these places and others besides.

After Asoka's death, about 236 B.C., the empire slipped away from his successors, though for 50 years Mauryans kept their hold on the Ganges Valley region. The Greek rulers in Bactria, having broken free from the Seleucid Empire, overran most of the Indus Valley early in the second century B.C. Next Parthians, then Scythians ("Sakas" in India), then oriental nomads, all in turn ruled in northwestern India. Elsewhere, the Mauryan Empire reverted to small principalities.

Asoka's support of Buddhism had spurred the Brahmans into revising the old Aryan faith. The ancient Dravidian cults were still very much alive, especially in the south. While the empire was breaking up, the Brahmans cleverly fused such Dravidian deities as Vishnu and Siva with their own Aryan gods. The result was a strong new faith, acceptable to both Aryan and Dravidian. This faith was later called Hinduism, "the religion of Hind (India)."

During the long period of political confusion, from about 200 B.C. to A.D. 300, Indian merchants capitalized on the trade opened up by Mauryan contacts. Three-masted ships carried Indian spices and muslins, precious stones and exotic pets like parrots, peacocks, monkeys and tigers to ports in the West to be traded for Roman pottery, glasswares and gold coins. Indian ships also went to Southeast Asia and China. This thriving trade stimulated an exchange of technical and artistic knowledge to the benefit of both East and West.

Top: birth of Buddha as visualized by a Tibetan artist. In the lower left corner he takes his first steps on a cross formed of circular blossoms. Asoka, a Hindu who was converted to Buddhism, helped spread this religion.

A *bodhisattva*, the ideal person or "saint" of Mahayana Buddhists. In this statue Graeco-Roman art styles (evident in the sensitively carved folds) mingle with Buddhist. This form of sculpture spread to China by the first century A.D. from Kushan and other Buddhist states in northwest India.

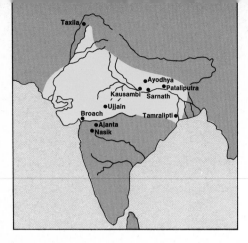

Top: Gupta Empire (yellow), towns and cities of Northern India and major rivers. During the Gupta period art and learning flourished in India. The territory of the Gupta emperors finally included all Northern India and part of Afghanistan.

Below: fifth century A.D. wall painting in an Ajanta cave showing a Buddhist monk. Ajanta paintings, which reveal the high level of artistic ability developed under the Guptas, influenced the art of Ceylon and central Asia.

The Gupta Dynasty

About A.D. 320, five centuries after the collapse of the Mauryan Empire, a new Chandragupta began to form an empire in Northern India. A series of military conquests and an advantageous marriage brought Chandragupta dominion over a large part of the Ganges Plain. This territory was further extended by his grandson, Chandragupta II, and eventually included all of northern India from the east to the west coast, as well as part of the Deccan region in the south. This second great Indian empire, ruled by the Gupta dynasty, lasted nearly 200 years.

Like the Mauryans, the Guptas had succeeded in unifying a multiplicity of small states. Unlike their predecessors, however, the Guptas never achieved a strong central control over these kingdoms. Many of the territories under Gupta influence continued to be ruled by their own princes, and some only paid tribute. Even those princes who were directly under the emperor's control were allowed to rule their own kingdoms, provided they had the aid and advice of imperial officials. These feudal princes, called *samantas*, were also expected to supply troops and attend the emperor on state occasions.

Under the Gupta dynasty, India experienced great peace and prosperity. Agricultural productivity was greatly increased by the addition of vast areas of newly-cleared land in the Ganges plain and the Deccan valleys. Trade increased, merchants and craft guilds prospered, and large cities like Pataliputra, Ayodhya and Kausambi grew rapidly in wealth and size. From the accounts of a Chinese Buddhist named Fa-hsein, who traveled to India about A.D. 405, we know that fifth-century India was also enjoying the benefits of just government, relative freedom from war, and remarkable reli-

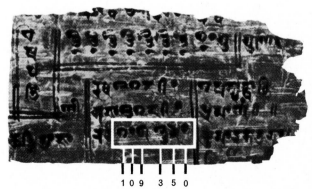

Above: Hindu numerals on a 12th century manuscript fragment. Indian mathematicians of the second and third centuries B.C. used a numeral system based on ten. About 1000 years ago the Arabs adopted these numerals and under the name "Arabic numerals" they gradually replaced Roman numbers in the West.

The unusual Ajanta caves, an early monastery abandoned in the seventh century A.D. From 200 B.C. Buddhists cut 28 caves into a sheer cliff which rises 250 feet above the river. Inside are many superb paintings done in lime overlaid on a clay, rice-husk and gum mixture plastered on rock.

gious toleration—Buddhism, Hinduism and Jainism were existing side by side without conflict.

It was a golden age in other respects, too. Poets, under the patronage of the merchants and princes, wrote verses in classical Sanskrit celebrating nature and love, singing the praises of the kings, and teaching morality, sometimes with sly humor. The outstanding poet-dramatist of the period was Kalidasa (about A.D. 400–455). His play *Sakuntala*, a comedy about the romance of a king and the daughter of a nymph, is still considered a masterpiece.

Imposing works of architecture and sculpture were also produced during this time. Buddhist craftsmen carved elaborate temples and monasteries out of the solid cliffs at Ajanta and Ellora. In the north, Hindu builders erected shrines and temples with curving sides, while in the south they built rectangular pyramids, each step of which was intricately carved to tell the story of some Hindu god. Vivid wall paintings, in the caves at Ajanta and elsewhere, also tell stories in pageants of vivid figures—princes and beggers, elephants and peacocks—as well as depicting many of the gods.

In Gupta times great strides were also made in the fields of medicine and the abstract sciences. Advances were made in the knowledge of human anatomy and the techniques of diagnosing disease. The astronomer Aryabhata (born A.D. 476) theorized that the spherical earth rotated around the sun. The mathematician Brahmagupta (born A.D. 598) extended studies in algebra and trigonometry.

About A.D. 600, Indian mathematicians also devised the system of nine numerals with zero, and began using decimals. This system, later adopted by the Arabs, in time reached the West.

The aesthetic and mystical aspect of Indian thought was expressed in new philosophies. *Vedanta*, one of the most important of the Hindu philosophies, rejected the objective world entirely, holding that the physical world was just a dream and that the only true reality was *Brahman*, the "Soul of the World." The goal of *yoga*, another Hindu development, was to free oneself of the body by gaining complete control over it. Only in this way could one ultimately be united with the universal soul.

During the fifth century, India was repeatedly invaded by Hun tribes from the northwest. As a result of these invasions, the Gupta dynasty fell about A.D. 500. When the Huns were finally driven out of India in the sixth century, no strong Indian leader came to the fore to rebuild the empire, but the Gupta culture lived on, even flourished, until the 11th century. At that time, the Moslems began to make forays over the northwestern mountain passes, foreshadowing an invasion which was to alter the course of Indian history.

Post-Mauryan pre-Gupta head of a *Tirthankara* (a Jain or Hindu savior). This sculpture illustrates cultural continuity at a time when India was politically disunited.

Islamic Rulers in India

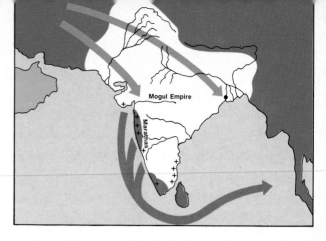

Main Moslem thrusts into India and seaborne spread of Islamic culture and ideas to Indonesia. The Marathas of west India began attacking the Mogul Empire in the 17th century. By this time the Europeans had set up trading posts along the southern coasts and were on the point of crushing Moslem power.

By A.D. 1000 Hinduism had so absorbed Buddhist elements that Buddhism had begun a permanent decline in India. But Hinduism was not to emerge as India's only religion. Islam was on the threshold, and it was armed.

In the early eighth century A.D., Moslem Arabs had installed themselves in the southwest Indus valley (Sind), occasionally raiding neighboring regions. The Hindus in general ignored them. In the early 11th century, a Turkish ruler launched 17 devastating assaults into northern India from Afghanistan, destroying temples and palaces, and returning to his capital (Ghazni) with slaves and idols, gold and jewelry. Still the northern kingdoms complacently concentrated on their own quarrels.

Mohammed of Ghor, another Turkish ruler in Afghanistan, led a large army through the Gomal Pass in 1192. This time the Hindu kingdoms did unite to face the Moslems, but Indian war elephants and outmoded tactics could not win the field against Turks and Afghans galloping to the attack on fast horses. The victors established the Delhi Sultanate, which was to dominate Northern India until the 16th century.

In 1325, the Turkish Sultan Mohammed Tughluk came to this throne with schemes to add the peninsular south to his empire. His resources, however, did not match his visions of aggrandisement. Before he died in 1351, even his own tax collectors had rebelled against his harsh rule, and the south was lost.

Less than 50 years later a new Moslem conqueror, the Mongol Timur, sped through the North. Timur killed 100,000 Hindu prisoners, pillaged Delhi, installed a governor in the Punjab, and then moved on to more important conquests. Former provinces of the vanquished Delhi Sultanate fought to regain their independence while a new Delhi kingdom was set up by Timur's representative in the Punjab. The result of Timur's brief year in India, however, was a general decentralization of power, and the consequent lessening of the Turkish and Afghan threat to the southern provinces.

Then, in the early 16th century, Afghan nobles in the north made a crucial mistake: hoping to oust an oppressive sultan in Delhi, they sought the support of a descendant of Timur. Babar ("Tiger") graciously consented to descend on Northern India. The result was his establishment in 1526 of a Mongol empire (called "Mogul" in India), centered on the fertile northern plains. By the 17th century, the Moguls had unified all of India except the southern tip. There, the local rulers had always fought stubbornly to preserve their ancient tradition of independence. And they held the Moguls at bay as successfully as they had staved off other empire-builders from the north in the centuries before.

Emperor Akbar, greatest ruler of the Mogul Empire, inspecting building operations at Fathpur Sikri. This city, which he built in the Ganges valley, was abandoned after his death.

At its height the Mogul Empire was under severe pressure. Portuguese and English traders had colonized points on the Indian shores, and forceful Hindu rulers, the Marathas, were too strong to be crushed. The Sikhs, too, became a threat. This religious order, which rejected the caste system, was founded by the *guru* ("teacher") Nanak (1469–1538). Nanak's message was that the god of the Moslems and the gods of the Hindus were all fundamentally one God. By the 18th century, the Sikhs were a dedicated military group.

At this time, the Hindu and Moslem religions were existing side by side, albeit resentfully. Circumstances had made some tolerance of Hinduism essential for Turkish rulers, because the Hindus were needed to serve in the armies. Even so, Hindus considered the caste-less Moslems to be unclean barbarians. The Moslems, in their turn, thought of the Hindus as contemptible idol worshipers and occasionally Hindu temples were violated. For most of the eight centuries of Moslem political domination, however, the two religions merely avoided conflict, while in customs, architecture and language there was interchange.

High-caste Hindus adopted the Moslem custom of *purdah*, for example, isolating their women from public view. Both the Hindus and the Moslems altered their dress, so that a Moslem woman might choose to wear a long Hindu skirt or a northern Hindu the voluminous pants of the Persians and Turks. A new language was evolved, called *Urdu*, which uses Persian and Arabic words and a grammar like that of Hindi.

Artists and architects mixing Persian and Indian styles pruduced subtle, richly colored miniatures and buildings with Persian arches and elaborate Indian decoration. Perhaps the most exquisite example of Moslem architecture anywhere in the world is the Taj Mahal (built 1632–1653), a mausoleum built for the favorite wife of the Mogul ruler Shah Jahan. Both the love lyric, and the use of bowed and plucked string instruments were introduced by the Persians, who in time adopted aspects of Indian mathematics and astronomy.

Babar and his army saluting their battle standards by sprinkling them with *kumiss* (an intoxicating liquor made of fermented mare's or camel's milk). First Mogul Emperor and grandfather of Akbar, Babar invaded India from Afghanistan in 1526 and defeated the Sultan of Delhi. Babar was related to Genghis Khan.

Top: eighth century Javanese carving of ships with outriggers.

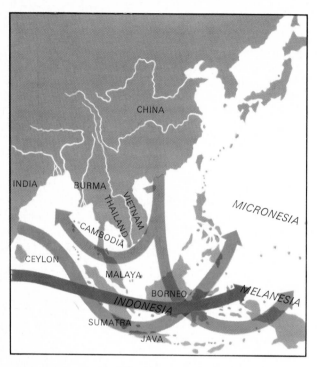

Above: map of Southeast Asia showing some of the major movements of peoples that, throughout history, have made this part of the world a meeting place of different cultures (Indians—blue arrow, Arabs—green arrow, and Chinese—red arrows).
Below: Japanese scroll painting of 1293 depicts a 13th-century Mongol invasion of Java. At this time the whole of the Far East was threatened by the new Mongol dynasty in China, but the Mongols never gained a foothold in the islands of southeast Asia.

Between India and China a long peninsula extends southeastward, its thrust continued by the islands that string out toward Australia and New Zealand. Long ago this mountainous area was a meeting place of different peoples and cultures. These included Negrito pygmies, Negroid Melanesians, and Mongoloids. On the peninsula, the Negrito hunters lived in the dense tropical jungles that blanketed high mountains. The others were farmers, who grew rice and soybeans in the lowlands and river deltas, and raised pigs, chickens and water buffalo.

Sometime before 1000 B.C. most of the Negritos migrated south. They crossed the sea from island to island, some of them eventually reaching Australia. A different people, now called Polynesians, also migrated before 1000 B.C. These were farmers and fishermen from South China, who probably left to avoid pressures from the organized Shang kingdom of the Yellow River basin (p. 122).

The Polynesians crossed vast expanses of unknown ocean. Some settled in Melanesia and Micronesia, but others sailed thousands of miles outward into Oceania, to the islands of the mid-Pacific. It seems impossible for a people at the New Stone Age level to have accomplished it, yet they knew how to build double canoes and outriggers, and could maneuver these large crafts under sail.

The people who stayed on the peninsula and the closer islands developed much faster because of their proximity to the advanced cultures of India and China. Tradition places Buddhist missions in Cambodia and Indonesia in the third century B.C. After the first century A.D., Western trade made the spices, gems, ivory and scented woods of southeast Asia valuable commodities for Indian and Chinese merchants. Ships plying between India and China stopped in Southeast Asia along the way, sometimes dropping off Buddhist and Hindu missionaries. Trading colonies were founded by Indians in Burma, Thailand, Cambodia, Java and Sumatra. The Chinese in the meantime were settling the Malay peninsula and Annam.

After A.D. 600, strong states appeared in Burma, Cambodia, Sumatra and Java. Cambodia is re-

ferred to in Chinese records of the early seventh century. The king of this state was considered a god and acted as the chief priest. Religion was the central focus of Cambodian life. In this and in language, the influence of India is clear. By the sixth century, Hinduism had overshadowed the old religion of the Cambodians, or Khmers, and Sanskrit was made the official language.

When the Khmer kingdom was at its most powerful (11th and 12th centuries A.D.), it included present-day Cambodia, Thailand, and southern Laos. Its fabulous capital, Angkor, had been built in the ninth century. In the mid 12th century, a temple, Angkor Wat, was erected nearby. This structure, with five acorn-shaped towers and bas-reliefs, making nearly every surface a mass of inticate forms, was a Hindu place of worship and a mausoleum for King Suryavarman II.

East of the Khmer Empire was Champa (probably corresponding to part of South Vietnam). Champa served as a buffer between Annam and Cambodia. The Chams themselves were hostile to Cambodia. They sacked Angkor in 1177 but Cambodia recovered from this blow.

The wide-ranging Mongols by 1300 A.D. had subdued Nan-Chao in Central Asia (p. 130) and Burma. They failed to take Java and did not attack Cambodia. The Mongoloid Thai peoples of Nan-Chao, however, moved south and brought a new force into the peninsula. In the 14th century Thailand was an independent kingdom strong enough to mount several invasions against the Khmer state. In 1450 the Cambodians retreated to the isolated south, and the jungle gradually reclaimed Angkor.

Early in the 15th century, Chinese emperors sent an armada westward, forcing many Southeast Asian states to pay tribute. By 1500, Moslem Arabs, through military might and religious conversion, had spread the faith of Islam to Malaya, Sumatra and Java, eclipsing Hinduism in those areas. In 1511 the Portuguese captured Malacca. The Chinese had lost interest in Southeast Asia by now, but the Europeans—Portuguese, Dutch, English and French—were very interested indeed.

Top: west entrance to Angkor Wat near Angkor, ancient capital of the Khmer Empire. This 12th century temple has a pyramidal form with a great bas-relief on its outer wall depicting extracts from Hindu stories and scenes from the life of King Suryavarman.

Below: artist's impression of a 13th century Arab ship. Though the Moslems had for long traded with Southeast Asia, it was not until the 13th century (chiefly under the influence of Indian Moslems) that Islam really began to establish itself there.

Map showing chief physical features and major rivers of China. It also indicates the extent of Shang influence (circling black lines) north of the Tsinling range between the Yellow and Yangtze Rivers (early centers of Chinese culture). Rulers of the Shang dynasty built Anyang, their capital city.

Chinese characters carved on an antler of the Chou period (11th–3rd century B.C.) Hundreds of years before this the Chinese had scratched records on bone. Although the horn is horizontal, the characters are read vertically.

About 15,000 B.C. tribes of nomads roamed the vast natural land mass of East Asia, an area stretching from the Pacific Ocean to the mountains of Tibet and from the cold deserts of Mongolia to the steaming forests of Southeast Asia. The nomads, a mongoloid people with straight black hair, round heads and slanting eyes, may have been the descendants of a much earlier people, whose presence in China some 400,000 years ago is indicated by the remains of prehistoric Peking Man.

Legendary Chinese history begins in 2953 B.C. with the Three Rulers and Five Emperors, and continues with the H'sia dynasty (2207–1766 B.C.). It is evident that before 2000 B.C. nomad tribes had begun to settle in the valleys and plains of both north and south China. In the south, where the subtropical climate allowed two or three harvests a year, they grew rice, while in the north, in the Yellow River Valley, they grew wheat and learned to increase their harvests through land drainage. The people of this northern region may have developed political organization early as a result of cooperative ventures in flood control and irrigation. That they had also profited from contact with the older cultures of West Asia is indicated by their knowledge of wheat cultivation, bronze tools and horsedrawn chariots.

In this valley the Shang dynasty (1766–1122 B.C.) rose to power and established dominion over an area slightly larger than Maryland. Shang rulers maintained control over this kingdom through the feudal system of granting land in exchange for services.

The peasants who farmed the nobles' land grew wheat, rice and millet, and raised pigs, sheep, cattle and horses. They lived in thatched huts and farmed with stone tools. Expensive bronze was reserved for the spears, arrows and axes used in war and for the possessions of the nobility.

Bronze was not the only luxury enjoyed by the nobles at court. Sericulture, the process of making silk from the cocoon of the silkworm, provided them with rich clothing; and Shang artists labored to produce ornamental works in ivory and marble for them. The art of the Shang period already showed the marks of formal simplicity and superb craftsmanship which were later to make Chinese art prized everywhere in the world.

The Shang people worshipped both nature spirits and the spirits of their ancestors. All these were honored and propitiated in sacrificial rituals presided over by the Shang priests, who also served as scribes. Bones inscribed with pictographs, the earliest form of Chinese characters, have been found by archeologists at Anyang, the town which became the Shang capital in 1300 B.C.

About 1122 B.C. the Shang kingdom was invaded and conquered by the Chou peoples, nomadic tribes from the northwest. Under the Chou dynasty which followed, an empire was forged which eventually included a large portion of northern China and some of its central region. But although the Chou dynasty ruled with a firm hand on its accession to the throne, the Chou kings had lost real control of the empire to the feudal barons before 256 B.C. By the early fifth century B.C., the continual struggle for power had led to the emergence of seven independent aggressive kingdoms, called the Warring States: Ch'in, Ch'i, Yen, Wei, Han and Chao.

Oddly enough, the civil strife and uncertainty of this period did not preclude economic and cultural progress. More land was cultivated and food production increased as a result of the mass-production

Top: mounted archer from a design stamped on a tile of the Chou period. Throughout China's history nomad hordes harried the northern frontiers. This horseman is firing a so-called "Parthian shot" over the rump of his animal.

Left: three Chinese philosophers, Shaka, Confucius and Lao-tzu. Confucius, the most famous of Chinese thinkers, and Lao-tzu began two great Chinese cultural traditions. Lao-tzu, traditional founder of Taoism, believed in the simplicity and humility of man. Confucius in his search for goodness stressed the "filial" relationship between ruler and subject.

of cast-iron tools for clearing the forests and tilling the soil. Manufacturers and merchants grew rich from the new cast-iron industry and the introduction of minted money.

It was during this period that a number of China's great philosophers lived and taught. Confucius (about 551–479 B.C.), Mencius (fourth century), and Lao-tzu (fifth and fourth centuries) sought, in different ways, to arrive at a code of ethics that would bring about individual and social harmony. Each was opposed to violence and concerned with the attainment of virtue and wellbeing. Confucius' philosophy advocated a way of life reminiscent of that which existed in the security and established tradition of early Chou rule. Lao-tzu stressed the necessity for universal love. The Taoists (from *Tao*, meaning "the way") urged that Man return to the simple goodness of his own nature.

A later group, however, who called themselves the Legalists, held that man's nature was essentially selfish and that only through strict laws and their strict enforcement could a stable society be achieved. Legalism's emphasis on strong central government made it the logical choice for the fundamental doctrine of a rising new political power, Ch'in.

Bronze drinking vessel of the Shang period. Before China felt the impact of the art styles of southwest Asia and the east Mediterranean, bronze vessels were one of the earliest and commonest Chinese art forms. The geometric decoration and tripodlike structure are typical of Chinese culture.

Early Chinese Empires

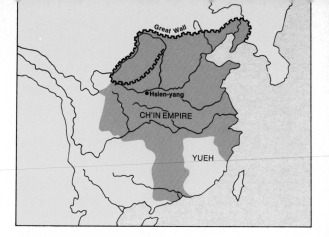

Map showing the limits of the Ch'in Empire. Under Ch'in rulers China's political boundaries began to assume their present-day shape. The barbaric mountain tribes in the southwest and the Yüeh people in the southeast were still independent. The massive Great Wall guarded the empire's northern frontiers.

The rulers of Ch'in, the westernmost of the seven Warring States, put the tenets of Legalism (p. 123) to work in establishing and maintaining control over their kingdom. They did away with the treacherous feudal system and ruled instead through a hierarchy of paid civil servants, selected on the basis of merit. They were generous in rewarding their people for bravery in battle and service to the state; they were ruthless in punishing both lawbreakers and idlers. Emphasis on law and governmental efficiency greatly strengthened the state.

Above: rubbing from a decorated brick of the Han period, dating from the first or second century A.D. Archers (right) hunt while "miners" (left) drill for brine.

At the same time, the clearance of large areas of forest for farming, and the construction of a vast irrigation system greatly increased agricultural productivity.

Ch'in, both prosperous and powerful, then turned to conquest. In the short space of nine years (230 to 221 B.C.) its armies stormed and took most of the remainder of China. Ch'in became an empire (and gave its name, in the process, to a whole succession of Chinese empires). The king who ruled Ch'in at the time made himself "First Emperor" *(Shih-huang-ti)* and proceeded to impose on his new territories the governmental system which already functioned so well in Ch'in.

Feudal barons were everywhere demoted in favor of imperial appointees who were installed as governors of 36 districts. An imperial code of laws was instituted, and weights and measures, writing, and money systems were standardized throughout the empire. Roads were built to connect the various parts of the empire and an impressive array of palaces and other buildings was erected at the capital city, Hsien-yang.

Criticism of the government was outlawed. To ensure right-thinking, the First Emperor burned all books he considered subversive. Furthermore, all private weapons were gathered in and melted down; only the state could authorize arms.

The nomadic Hsiung-nu (Hun) tribes were a serious threat to the Ch'in empire in the north. To secure defense against these tribes, the First Emperor ordered the building of a lengthy fortified wall along the northern boundary of the empire. The Great Wall, an expansion and strengthening of existing barriers, was almost 1400 miles long by 214 B.C. To build this wall millions of men were conscripted by the government. So many died in the task that the Great Wall has been described as the longest graveyard in the world.

The First Emperor had believed that the unification and strict regulation of China would prevent civil war. About 206 B.C., however, the overworked conscriptees, joined by the intellectuals, rose against

Part of a tomb relief dating from A.D. 147. The linked balls represent the Big Dipper (a cluster of seven stars) bearing a government official.

Great Wall of China, composed of granite blocks, clay bricks and rammed earth. This structure, the longest ever built, sprawls across northern China for more than 1400 miles. 25 feet wide at the base and 15 feet at the top, the wall has a road running along it and small fortified towers placed at regular intervals. Reports say that one in every three able-bodied Chinese was mobilized by the Ch'in rulers to link and extend existing short defensive walls.

the First Emperor's son, and the Ch'in dynasty came to an end. In 202 B.C., a new dynasty, the Han, was founded by a commoner, Liu Pang.

The Han dynasty controlled China for four centuries, with only one 15-year interruption (A.D. 9–23), provided by Wang Mang, regent for a child emperor, who attempted to found a new dynasty.

The Han period reached its zenith under the emperor Han Wu-ti (140–87 B.C.). This "Martial Emperor" concentrated on military achievement. Under his leadership, the Han armies roundly defeated the Hsiung in the north and took part of Korea. Conquests in the south included the kingdoms of the Yüeh; Han troops also pushed west into Central Asia.

These conquests brought China rich new lands for colonization. They also brought the opening of important trade routes, particularly that of the famous Silk Road between China and Persia.

Wu-ti's military conquests strengthened the empire and increased its trade. But both his armies and his civil service were expensive, and to afford them, he had to increase taxes, confiscate estates,

sell titles, and make state monopolies of the prosperous salt and iron industries.

During the Ch'in and Han dynasties, numerous important cultural and economic advances were made; the many inventions and developments included porcelain, papermaking, sundials and water clocks. The use of fertilizer and the clearing of new lands again increased harvests. By A.D. 2, the population had risen to about 50 million people.

When the last Han emperor was forced, by powerful generals, to abdicate the throne in A.D. 220, the empire was divided into separate units.

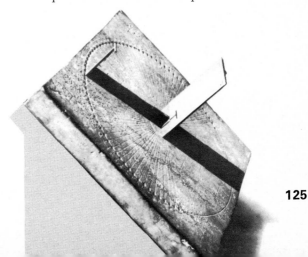

Limestone sundial dating from the second century B.C., probably designed to tell the season as well as the time of day. During the late Han period science, learning and art thrived.

125

T'ang China

Larger-than-life size figure of an *Arhat* (Buddhist disciple) modeled in clay and covered with white, green and brown glazes. Early in the T'ang period sculptured figures became more life-like, possibly because of new contacts with India and central Asia.

After the collapse of the Han dynasty (p. 125) the weakness of a politically-divided China encouraged invasion by the barbarians in the north and east. Tribes of Huns, Turks and Tibetans repeatedly attacked and finally devastated China in the fourth century A.D. When at last they settled down to rule the territories they had conquered, they realized their lack of administrative experience and this forced them to accept the existing Chinese methods of government. The barbarians began by using Chinese administrative procedures and soon were taking Chinese names and Chinese brides.

The powerful Sui family was the product of one of these Chinese-barbarian marriages. The Sui attained power and set about reuniting China in the years A.D. 581–589. They reconquered the fertile southern kingdoms and rebuilt the Great Wall to secure the north against further barbarian invasions. They also built a canal connecting the Yangtze and the Yellow rivers, in order that the Chinese armies protecting the north might receive shipments of rice from the productive southern provinces.

The canal project was accomplished with great speed by millions of laborers forced by conscription to leave their families and farms. The resentment of these conscriptees was echoed by that of the soldiers, who were opposed to the emperor's costly and unsuccessful attempts to conquer Korea and crush the northwestern Turks. Out of this resentment a widespread rebellion developed, which ultimately resulted in the death of the Sui emperor and the establishment of the new T'ang dynasty (A.D. 618–907).

Under the T'angs, China enjoyed three centuries of strong government. T'ang methods of taxation, finance, law and defense worked so well that they came to be imitated by both Korea and Japan. The T'ang emperors significantly improved the civil service system by requiring both aspirants-to-office and office-holders to take qualifying examinations. Government jobs and promotions were given to men of real ability. Because the examination system left less room for the exercise of "privilege" in government, it tended to produce a corps of officials whose first allegiance was to the emperor rather than to any one influential family.

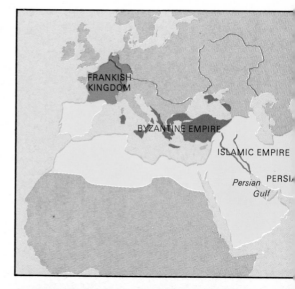

Top: part of the Buddhist *Diamond Sutra*, the world's oldest surviving printed book made in A.D. 868. Formed of printed sheets pasted end to end, it makes a scroll 16 feet long.

Below: eighth century empires. This map disproves the popular belief that civilizations in the East and West developed in complete isolation. The Chinese T'ang Empire stretched across central Asia to the Islamic world, where ideas and art styles were exchanged. Chinese inventions like paper making spread first to Islam and from there to Europe.

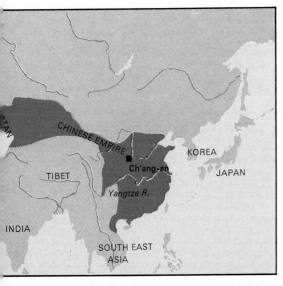

During the period of T'ang rule, China also achieved great military and economic strength. Two seventh-century rulers, T'si-tsung and Kao-tsung, finally succeeded in the conquest of Korea and Central Asia, and by the eighth century even the emerging nation of Tibet was under China's aegis. Meanwhile, the southern provinces were producing ever-larger crops, land-clearance and building were in progress throughout the empire, and the capital city, Ch'ang-an, numbered its inhabitants at almost a million. Trade flourished as a result of the reopening of the overland silk routes, and Chinese junks sailed to ports in Japan, Korea, Southeast Asia, India and the Persian Gulf.

The T'ang empire reached its cultural zenith during the reign of Emperor Hsüan-tsung (A.D. 712–756). Himself a patron of the arts, the emperor often received such poets as Li Po and Wang Wei at court. Landscape and figure painters, story-writers and lyric poets, sculptors, metalworkers, potters and architects produced works of consummate skill and beauty during this time. Nor were inventors and technicians idle: it was during this period that such innovations as tea-cultivation, clockwork, gunpowder, block printing, mapmaking, coal-burning, the water mill and the wheel-barrow made their first appearance.

Religion played an important role as a medium of cultural exchange. Buddhist monks from India, Zoroastrian and Manichaean missionaries from Persia, and Nestorian Christians from the West had made their way to China by the seventh century. In addition to the teachings of their various faiths, they brought with them the scientific knowledge and artistic traditions of their own cultures.

A series of disasters in the eighth and ninth centuries preceded the final collapse of T'ang China. The Arabs took Turkestan in 751. A huge rebel force, led by the Chinese governor of a northern province, rose against the empire and wrought enormous destruction from 755 to 757. Tibetan tribes sacked Ch'ang-an, the capital, in 763. Manichaean, Nestorian, Buddhist and Zoroastrian sects were ruthlessly persecuted by the Taoist emperor Wu-Tsung from 841 to 846. And from 874 to 883, famine and high taxes drove peasants to join a growing band of plunderers who savagely attacked the rich and prosperous.

A T'ang general finally dispersed these bandits, but was powerless to prevent a growing civil war among the provinces. In 907, the last T'ang emperor abdicated and the empire fell into disunity.

An exquisite example of T'ang art. Part of a landscape painted by Li Ssu-hsün (A.D. 651–716). His objective style with sparkling blue, green and gold colors reflects the pomp of the T'ang court.

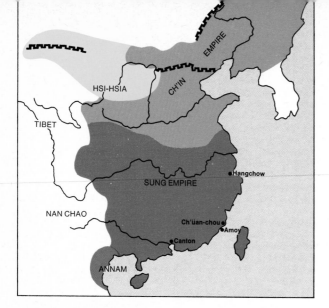

Top: map of China in the mid 12th century showing the Ch'in Empire in the north, Hsi Hsia ("western Hsia") and the Sung Empire with its four main cities. The Hsia barbarians were mainly Tibetan in origin. Broken line indicates stretches of wall defenses.

A lively detail from *Going up the River for the Spring Festival* by the artist Chang Tse-tuan. Painted about 1125, this scene of traders and travelers crowding across a bridge recreates the colorful life of Pien-lang (modern Kaifeng), capital of Sung China.

Sung China

For more than 50 years after the fall of the T'ang dynasty, fragmented China was a battleground for rival warlords and generals. But in A.D. 960 a leader emerged who was strong enough to enforce re-unification. He was T'ai-tse, founder of the Sung dynasty (960–1279), who with his successor, T'ai-tsung, set about establishing firm rule in the south. The north was entirely in the hands of "barbarians," the warlike Khitan Mongols, whose territory included not only Inner Mongolia and southern Manchuria, but also a large area within the Great Wall. Yen-chou (Peking) became the Khitan capital in 936; the series of Khitan kings was known as the Liao ("Iron") dynasty.

Although the early Sung emperors were sufficiently martial to restore southern unity, they were unable to regain the lost northern territories from the Liao. Nor were their armies, despite their fearsome "fire cannon," any more successful against the Jurchens, another mongoloid tribe, who conquered the Liao state in the 12th century and founded in its place the Chin ("golden") dynasty. So the north remained barbarian, the Sung emperors finding it much easier to appease their aggressive neighbors than to fight them. The tribute paid to the Jurchens was enormous; tens of thousands of silver taels and bolts of silk had to be paid them yearly.

Danger also threatened on other borders. To the northwest was Hsi Hsia (Western Hsia), a Tibetan kingdom which extorted tribute from the Sung; to the southwest were the equally hostile states of Nan-Chao and Annam.

Unable to subdue these aggressive neighbors, the Sung emperors could still dismiss them as barbarians and deplore their way of life. There was little glory to be won in defeating such uncivilized opponents. The Sung preferred to buy them off and so win time for intellectual and cultural pursuits. These were of far greater importance to the Sung than martial triumph and brutal conquest.

Internally, however, the Sung reigned with a firm hand. The control which these scholar-statesmen exercised over their country was maintained by an expanded and improved civil service. Examinations were held more frequently and the number of candidates increased. Those who were successful received an immediate grant of money, even if no vacancies were awaiting them; those who did serve the state were rewarded with high salaries and grants of land. The highest honors went to those who passed the most difficult examinations.

This system greatly strengthened imperial authority because the aristocrats, finding that "privilege" counted less and less in the state hierarchy, had far fewer opportunities for successfully challenging the emperor's power. Gradually they abandoned their court intrigues and instead became landed gentry, living off estates managed by bailiffs and worked by tenants and slaves.

The Sung regard for intellectual and cultural accomplishments set the tone of the age. Philosophers, historians, poets, ceramicists and painters were unusually productive. Landscape painting, in particular, made great advances. In the hands of celebrated writers like Ssu-ma Kuang (1019–1086) literature flourished. The first of the great Chinese encyclopedias was compiled under the emperor's personal supervision.

This was an age of innovation, too, in which the Sung devised the magnetic compass and enthusiastically adopted the Korean invention of movable type for printing. Some of the first novels, based on plays and story tellers' tales, were now being written and printed.

Nourished by buoyant trade and commerce, which could now be financed with paper money lent on interest, the cities grew and prospered. Under the Sung emperors Hangchow became the the largest city in the world. Among the busiest and richest cities were Ch'üan-chou, Amoy and Canton, whose harbors were crowded with ships and merchants from as far west as Mesopotamia.

By the end of the 11th century the population of the south had trebled (the combined population of Chin and Sung China at this time totaled about 100 million). This huge increase was made possible by an immense rise in food production, the result of large-scale land reclamation and the use of better farm methods and quick-ripening wheat.

But for many life was still hard. In the country the practice of buying and selling tenants and their lands brought suffering to millions.

Nevertheless the Sung state was, for the most part, a stable, cultured, and prosperous society. Its greatest weakness was the inability of its rulers to secure it from the determined assault of a people whom eventually neither taels nor silk could buy off—the Mongols.

Top: *Noble Scholar under a Willow,* an 11th century masterpiece in ink and colors on silk. Many Sung artists and scholars gave up public positions and became recluses.

Delicate black and white vase (Tz'u Chou ware) of the Sung dynasty. During Sung rule Chinese porcelain and silks were shipped to Japan in the east and Egypt in the west.

The Mongol Empire

Above: 13th century Japanese scroll painting commemorates an unsuccessful Mongol invasion. The exploding bomb is an example of the advanced war techniques the Mongols learned from the Chinese.

On the steppes of Central Asia, hundreds of miles northwest of China's Great Wall (p. 124), lived the Mongol and Turkish nomads. These groups of illiterate wanderers, once they united, were to conquer more of the world than any conquerers before them—and in a span of less than 100 years.

The geography of their homelands encouraged toughness and belligerence. They lived their nomad life in an area bordered by high mountain ranges in and by the Siberian forests in the north. Much of it is too dry or cold for settled agriculture, but water and pasturage were enough to support the roving mongoloid herdsmen. Their livestock (sheep, camels and cattle) supplied most of their needs: meat and milk, warm clothing, transportation, and shelter too, for their circular tents were made from wool felt. The nomads depended on their fast horses for hunting and warfare. The nomads were renowned for their expert horsemanship and archery.

Over the centuries, Asia, Europe, the Middle East and India had suffered from the hit-and-run attacks of the nomadic Huns, Turks, Tibetans and others. In all these areas the nomads had earned a reputation for savagery, but it is also true that at first they did not embark on raids simply to indulge a taste for brutality. When pastures suddenly dried up or an epidemic struck their animals, they had to seek plunder in order to survive. Usually, after their onslaught, the Mongol nomads withdrew or were absorbed by the peoples they had invaded.

In the 13th century, however, a warring Mongol chief named Temuchin began a career of conquest for its own sake. By 1206, having conquered all the tribes in his vicinity, he had taken the name Genghis Khan, "Very Mighty King."

Genghis Khan was intoxicated with conquest. His army was small but thoroughly organized and disciplined, and he himself was a brilliant military strategist. Under his leadership, the hardy nomad warriors swept through the civilized world: north-

ern China, northern Persia, southern Russia and Hsi Hsia (p. 128). Genghis Khan died in 1227 during the siege and capture of the capital of Hsi Hsia.

Two of the Very Mighty King's successors, the "Great Khan" Ogodei (1229–1241) and Kublai (1260–1294), made the name of Mongol ring from sea to sea. The Chinese Sung Empire (p. 128) resisted Kublai for four and a half years but fell at last in 1273. With the addition of Sung China, the Mongol Empire stretched from the Pacific Ocean to the Black Sea.

The empire reached its greatest size during the reign of Kublai Khan. It was so extensive that the Mongols divided it into four parts, or *Khanates*. The Great Khan, Kublai, ruled the East Asian lands from Cambaluc. The three other Khanates, ruled by Khans responsible to the Great Khan, were Afghanistan and Turkestan; Persia and other Near East conquests; and western Asia, Russia and the Ukraine (the khanate known as the Golden Horde). In all the Khanates, the Mongols set up orderly governments run by a huge civil service.

The Great Khan was also emperor of China. Kublai was the first emperor of this new dynasty in

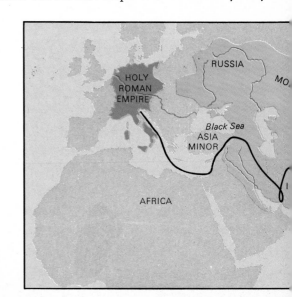

Tamerlane (Timur the Lame) receiving Bayezid I, the defeated sultan of the Ottoman Turks, after the battle of Ankara in 1402. A Mongol Turk descended from Genghis Khan, Tamerlane forged a huge but short-lived empire. From 1369 his armies thrust west into Persia and Asia Minor and south into Afghanistan and India.

Mongol Empire in the late 13th century. Expanding from their homeland (dark circle), Mongol warriors overran most of central Asia and invaded eastern Europe. However, stable Mongol rule enabled explorers like Marco Polo (route arrowed) to travel extensively in central and eastern Asia.

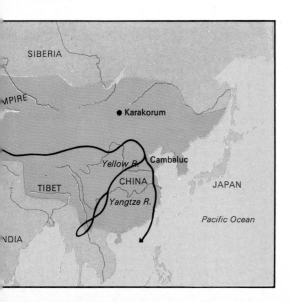

China, the Yuan dynasty. Kublai emerges from history as a humane, intelligent man. Other Mongols, however, detested intellectuals and persecuted them. The Chinese, in particular, were discriminated against; in their own country they were legally inferior to Persians, Turks, Arabs and others, according to the caste system the Mongols imposed.

With all of Central Asia under one strong government, trade and travel between East and West increased. A traveler from Venice, Marco Polo, served Kublai for 17 years (1275–1292), making journeys on his behalf in China, Southeast Asia and Southern India. His later accounts of the magnificence of East Asia astonished the Western World.

The Mongol Empire lasted less than a century. In the west the khans campaigned against one another; in the east Asian khanate, Mongol power was weakened by difficulties over the succession. By 1371 the Yüan dynasty had been overthrown by a new Chinese dynasty and the Mongols pushed back.

While this was happening in China, a forceful Mongol in Turkestan was gaining supremacy over the other khans. This "Prince of Destruction," Timur Lenk (Tamerlane), almost managed to reestablish the Mongol Empire under one rule, but his death in 1405, while en route to China, put an end to this possibility.

Japanese Civilization

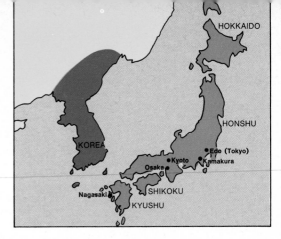

Map of Japan and Korea. From the 17th century for almost 200 years Japanese rulers, fearing European infiltration and foreign domination, isolated their country from the rest of the world. The Japanese were not allowed to leave their homeland and only a few foreign ships a year were permitted to enter Japanese ports.

Sometime in the sixth millennium B.C. men were living in Japan, an arc of islands about 1350 miles long. The earliest inhabitants were probably Ainus, a hairy, fair-skinned group whose descendants now live on the island of Hokkaido. Another people, who became the dominant group, were Mongoloids. They had arrived in southwest Japan from Korea by the second century B.C., bringing with them a language from Northwest Asia. There are also indications of Southeast Asian influence—in the ancient legends of Japan and in the methods used by the early Japanese to build houses. These settlers began growing rice in cultivated fields and fishing along the coasts.

The proximity of Korea, located about 100 miles from the southern islands of Japan, brought some early contact between the two peoples. From the Koreans, the Japanese acquired knowledge of iron and bronze tools, and also of a religion of nature- and ancestor-worship. During long periods of isolation, the Japanese were to develop this religion in a unique way. Eventually *Shinto* ("Way of the Spirits") provided a religious background for emperors, who were regarded as descendants of the sun goddess Amaterasu.

Ancient Japan was governed by clan chiefs ruling as representatives of their clan gods. By the fifth century A.D. these leaders were exerting feudal control over most of southern Japan. By this time, too, a clan chief had come forward as emperor above the others. With the combined might of the feudal armies, Japan subdued southern Korea.

During the Japanese occupation of Korea, which lasted until A.D. 633, contact was made with Chinese ideas and techniques. Chinese and Chinese-taught Koreans traveled to Japan, where they introduced improved metalworking techniques, silk manufacture, and methods of making pottery. Chinese scribes arrived and by the eighth and ninth centuries, the Chinese script had been adapted for use in writing the Japanese language. Japanese painters, sculptors, and architects were stimulated and influenced by the styles of the T'ang dynasty (p. 126). Buddhist monks and scholars from the mainland converted many important Japanese to Buddhism, and large Buddhist monasteries were built.

Japanese emperors bolstered their authority by adopting important aspects of the Chinese administration, including its civil service, its methods of tax collection, and even its laws. To some extent these measures succeeded in strengthening the central government, but in A.D. 858 a strong clan, the Fujiwara, seized control, and the emperor became a mere figurehead.

During the Fujiwara period no more envoys were sent to China. The Japanese looked inward until

Scene from the Battle of Shijo Nawate by 19th century artist Kunyioshi. At this battle, fought in 1348, the Ashikaga family defeated their rivals, the Kusunoki Clan. This painting commemorates one of the civil wars that racked feudal Japan in the 14th–16th centuries.

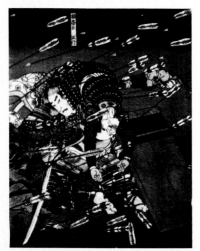

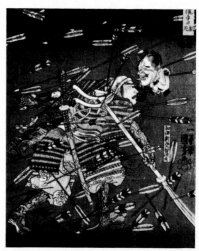

Top: Japanese artist's impression of a *Kabuki* theater. Developed in the 17th century, *Kabuki* is characterized by chanted narratives and speeches. The runway through the audience represents a road, and revolving stages, realistic scenery and music heightened the drama.

the 12th century. Clans and emperors won and lost power in civil wars until a central military government was set up in Kamakura in 1192. The emperor was nominally responsible for civil and religious affairs, but effective power was in the hands of military despots called shoguns (from *Seiidaisshogun*, "barbarian-subduing great general").

The rise of warriors to the ruling position in Japan was timely. A new outside influence was soon to make its impact in Japan. In 1280 the Mongols, already masters of China, expected the Japanese to become their subjects voluntarily. The Mongol envoys to Japan, however, were executed. In 1281 the Mongols sent 150,000 men against these impertinent islanders. On land, their mobility had always been the chief asset of Mongol horsemen, but at sea the Japanese, in smaller ships, had the advantage. Continually defeated by the Japanese ships, the Mongols were forced to withdraw altogether when a storm wrecked much of their fleet.

This was a marvelous victory for the Japanese, but until 1333 the shoguns struggled to overcome the strain that the defense of Japan had put on the economy. In 1331 civil war ended the First Shogunate and the Japanese entered a 200-year period of feudalism and anarchy.

Unification was finally accomplished by the shogun Tokugawa Ieyasu, who founded an efficient feudal regime which extended to all the island. Known as the Tokugawa period, the years 1600–1868 were marked by both peace and prosperity for the Japanese. Trade and commerce flourished and a large merchant class came into being. Richly illustrated books were printed. In the theater, a more active drama, called *Kabuki*, developed from the formal *Noh* and lyric drama of earlier centuries.

Left: eighth century *Gigaku* mask from Japan. Designed for use in Buddhist services, this mask formed part of religious ritual costumes. Indian and especially Chinese influences were strong. Many traditions forgotten in these countries still survive in this islanded Japan.

133

AFRICA

For a long time Europeans were content to dismiss Africa as "the Dark Continent," a land mass which had been left behind in man's forward march and one with no history to speak of. Today we know that the African peoples have a long history of social development and that there were flourishing civilizations in Africa, south of the Sahara, long before the great Age of Discovery.

Benin bronze "altar of the Hand." In the center is the Oba, king of Benin, holding a staff and gourd; above him is the queen holding two ceremonial swords and below the king are two hands. This altar was worshiped because of the hand's power of achievement. Metal casting was probably introduced into Benin from Ife during the 13th century.

Empires of West Africa

Long before the Europeans had real awareness of Africa, feudal states were emerging in the West African grasslands below the vast and forbidding Sahara Desert. The development of ironworking—the mining and smelting of iron ore for tools and weapons—was bringing great changes in the life of the West African village peoples. Tribes possessing the new metal conquered the weaker and less advanced tribes, forged kingdoms and empires, built cities, and began to engage actively in trade. Ghana, for instance, which became the first West African empire, owed its military successes to the use of iron weapons against the "bars of ebony" wielded by its neighbors.

Another vital factor in the emergence of the West African kingdoms was the presence of gold mines in the southern coastal areas of the grasslands and of salt deposits in the north. Gold led the Arab and Berber merchants of North Africa to pioneer trade routes across the Sahara and, by the 10th century A.D., they had secured a virtual monopoly of the caravan trade to Ghana. To the peoples *south* of the grasslands, on the other hand, salt was the precious mineral. To procure it, they were willing to pay its weight in gold. Ghana, at its height in the 10th and 11th centuries, and Mali, a kingdom which rose to greatness in the 14th century, became rich both through trade and through exacting tribute from every caravan which passed through their kingdoms. Among the great West African cities nourished by this trade were Timbuktu, which had begun as a settlement of nomads in the 11th century; Gao, the capital of Songhay; Kumbi Saleh, a capital of Ghana; and Djenné, which reached its greatest prosperity in the days of the Mali empire.

The North Africans' commercial interest in the resources of West Africa made them an important factor in the growth of these cities. When their

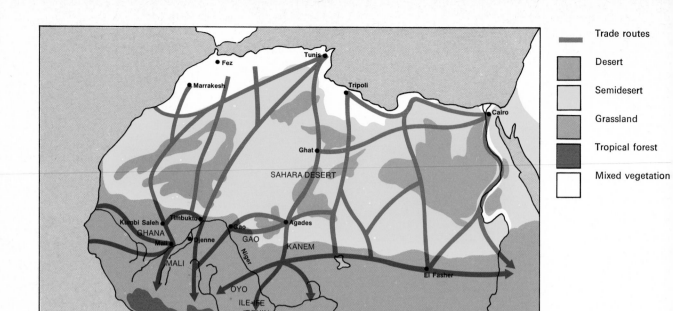

Map of medieval northern Africa showing natural vegetation, West African states, major towns and trade routes. A civilization had flourished and died in Egypt thousands of years before the development of West African empires like Mali, Kanem and Benin.

interest took a more violent form, however, it caused the rapid decline of at least one of them. In the 11th century, Kumbi Saleh had become so rich that it attracted plundering raids. A north African dynasty, the Almoravids (p. 106), who had already undertaken the spread of Islam to Ghana, sacked Kumbi in 1076. They were so thorough in their devastation that the empire was permanently weakened. A neighboring people soon completed the demise of the Ghana empire, preparing the way for Mali, which was to become the largest and most powerful of all West African kingdoms.

Islam, meanwhile, had found converts among West African rulers, in spite of the hostile acts of some North African Moslems. The most famous ruler of Mali, Gongo Musa (1307–1332), made a pilgrimage to Mecca. Mosques were built in Timbuktu, Djenné, and other cities, and there was so much interest in learning that the 16th-century traveler, Leo Africanus, reported that more profit was made in Timbuktu from the sale of books than from any other business.

Another traveler, Ibn Batuta, had already seen the cultures of India and China when he visited Mali in 1352–1353. He was greatly impressed by its people's devotion to Moslem ritual, but admired other characteristics even more. "Of all peoples," he said, "the Negroes most abhor injustice."

Terra-cotta head by 13th-century Yoruba artist used to decorate a sacrificial altar. About A.D. 1000 the Yoruba established a kingdom in the Niger lands, with Ife as the capital. The best work of Ife craftsmen in bronze, terracotta and brass ranks among the finest of primitive art.

Top: Golden death mask of King Kofi of Ashanti (Ghana). The Ashanti people were a strong military power in the 18th century; their wealth was based on their gold mines and profitable trans-Saharan trade with the Arabs.

Nevertheless, slavery, perhaps the greatest injustice of all, was an accepted fact in West Africa. It was common practice there, as it had been for centuries elsewhere in the world, to kill or enslave conquered peoples. Slaves were often sold, along with gold, ivory and pepper, to the North African traders. When ships from Portugal touched on the West African shore in the 15th century, slave-trading took a new and much more serious turn.

At the time when the Portuguese and other Europeans first began trading in West Africa, still another area—what is now southwest Nigeria—had developed advanced cultures. The work done in bronze, brass, and terra cotta by the sculptors of Ile-Ife and Benin was so sophisticated that it now stands among the finest examples of African art.

Trade between Europeans and the peoples of Benin, Oyo, Akwamu and other states began as a normal exchange of such goods as gold and ivory. The opening of lands in America and the West Indies, however, brought with it an increased demand for cheap labor, which soon began to be met with the purchase of slaves from West Africa. This traffic in people grew to major proportions, succeeding at last in depopulating West Africa more than the Black Plague had depopulated Europe, and robbing West Africa of its most important resource, its men, for centuries.

West African figure made of separate metal plates. The use of iron spread into West Africa just over 2000 years ago. This statue was probably placed in a shrine to Gu, god of iron and warfare—two important factors in medieval western Africa.

East African Cities and Ruins

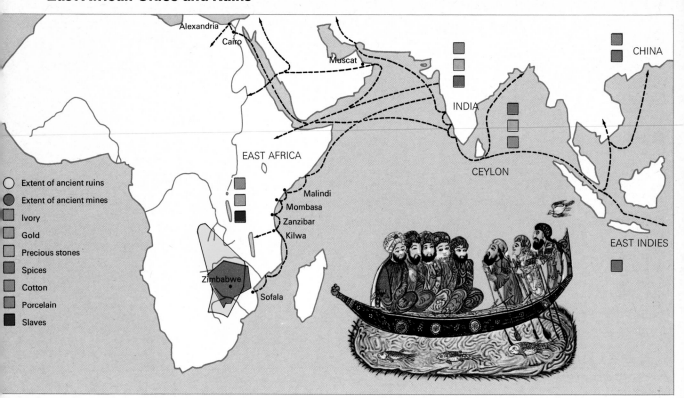

The east coast of Africa was enjoying the benefits of a thriving sea trade long before 1497, when Portuguese ships first sailed around the Cape of Good Hope and north into the Indian Ocean. Much to their surprise, the Portuguese found many large and prosperous ports and towns along the African coast. In the harbors they saw ships from the Far East and found pilots on whose skill and knowledge they could depend in setting their course northward. Where they had expected to find primitive tribal life, they found people who lived in well-built houses and who were accustomed to such luxury goods as Chinese porcelain and Indian jewelry.

Much of the original impetus for the busy trade and flourishing culture of this sea-coast civilization had come from the Arabs. As in West Africa (p. 135), Arab merchants had been the first to pioneer potentially rich trade routes. Arab traders had also settled in the coastal cities with which they traded, and the resulting interchange between the Arab and African cultures had given a distinctive quality to the developing civilization of the coast. One effect of Arab influence was the adoption by many east coast people of the Moslem religion. Another was the evolution of *Swahili*, a language which combines elements of both Arabic and native African tongues.

Although they were isolated from the coast, the peoples of the interior were also slowly developing

Top: map shows East Africa's role in the huge trading network of the Islamic world. Inset is a representation of an Arab trading vessel. Cities like Mombasa, probably founded by the Arabs in the 11th century, had trade links with Alexandria in Egypt, Muscat in Arabia and ports in far away India and China. The ruins of Zimbabwe in Rhodesia are relics of a civilization whose wealth was based on its mines, perhaps the empire of Monomotapa.

their own skills, arts and cultures. Some hunted or kept livestock for food, while others had learned to farm the tropical lands of east and central Africa.

About A.D. 1000 one of the inland groups, the people living in what is now Rhodesia, began mining gold and trading with the coastal cities. In exchange for goods from the East, these inlanders traded not only gold but also ivory, iron, slaves and animal skins. African iron was particularly valued by Indian traders, who bought it in large quantities.

Increased contact between the peoples of the interior and those of the coast helped stimulate progress inland. The peoples there began to build impressive stone palaces and forts like Great Zimbabwe (in present-day Rhodesia, about 17 miles southeast of Fort Victoria).

Scientific study, including radiocarbon dating of wood from the site, shows Zimbabwe was built not earlier than A.D. 1000. We also know that additions to the original buildings were being made

Top: Fort Jesus, Mombasa. This city was a thriving commercial center when the Portuguese arrived in the 15th century. When they built Fort Jesus (1593–1595), Mombasa was their capital in East Africa. In 1698 the fort was captured by the Arabs after an 18-month siege, the Portuguese relief fleet arriving 48 hours too late to prevent its fall.

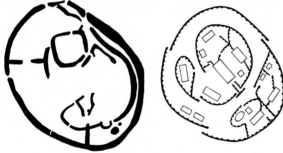

Above and below: ruins of ancient Zimbabwe. Top: high wall of great elliptical building made of granite blocks. Above: ground plans show similarity between Zimbabwe (left) and present-day mud-built African village. Below: aerial view of the ruins.

as late as the 18th century. There is proof here of a prosperous and well-organized African civilization.

The increasing wealth of the coastal cities was an irresistible attraction to the Portuguese, who early in the 16th century formed the habit of sailing into African ports and demanding tribute. Any port or city which refused their demands was instantly looted and burned. One by one the east coast towns fell; some were taken over by the Portuguese, others were wantonly destroyed. African trade with the Far East came to a halt.

Inevitably this was a severe blow to the prosperity of the interior. There people had also suffered from the incursions of the Portuguese, but the arrival of other Africans like the Zulus and Nguni was even more disastrous. Zimbabwe and other centers of civilization fell before the onslaught of the cruel tribal warriors, and their inhabitants were either massacred or driven out. The stage was left clear for European conquest and colonization.

THE AMERICAS

What were the Americas like before Columbus and other explorers crossed the Atlantic? Our knowledge of the early peoples of North and South America is still far from complete, but we do know that the ancient civilizations of Mexico and Peru are at least 3,000 years old. Even earlier were the migrations of the ancestors of the American Indians, and it is with these that this chapter begins.

Dignified Mandan Indians wearing ceremonial robes. Made of buffalo skin, these garments and moccasins were embroidered by the women using brightly colored porcupine quills. The men, proud of their decorative skill, painted their robes to show personal histories; how many enemies slain or hunts directed. The Mandans lived by hunting buffalo which were vital for clothing and food.

The American Indians

The first inhabitants of North America were a Mongolian people from East Asia. They began crossing the ice-covered Bering Strait into what is now Alaska perhaps more than 30,000 years ago. Then their descendants gradually moved south and east, eventually settling in the mountainous coastal areas of the west, the forest regions of the east and southeast, the wide central plains, and the desert regions of the southwest. Some continued moving south into Middle and South America. The wide differences in the physical characteristics, languages and customs of their descendants, who occupy these regions, indicate that these migrations took place over thousands of years.

Thanks to Indian legends and the patient work of modern archeologists, we can piece together something of the history of North America before Columbus arrived on the scene.

Indians of the eastern forest regions, which ranged from the Atlantic coastline to the Mississippi River, lived by hunting and fishing and farming. Among the most advanced of these Indians were the Mound Builders, skilled workers in stone, wood and copper, who settled in the Ohio and Mississippi valleys about the beginning of the Christian era. These people are known for their gigantic earthworks, often built in the shape of serpents or birds and variously described by archeologists as temples, temple foundations, or tombs.

Anthropologists believe that the successors to the Mound Builders were the Natchez, one of the Muskhogean-speaking nations of the southeast. They were talented pottery makers and weavers but, like all American Indians, never developed the plow or the wheel. The Natchez culture was dominated by a rigid caste system made up of three separate classes—nobles, freemen and slaves.

Another southeastern group, the Creek Indians,

Ruins of Mesa Verde, a Pueblo village clinging to a canyon wall in Colorado. This closely knit community of terraced dwellings made with adobe bricks was built 700 years ago. Today there are 20 000 Pueblo Indians, living in Arizona and New Mexico.

lived in towns of several thousand inhabitants. They developed a system of recording significant events in their history by means of strings of shells, whose arrangement served as a memory-jogger to the story-telling elders.

Farther north dwelt the Iroquois tribes who lived in villages of long bark-covered houses. The Iroquois succeeded in forming the only lasting and effective union of Indian tribes. Called the Five Nations (Mohawk, Cayuga, Oneida, Onondaga and Seneca), this confederacy helped the Iroquois meet and withstand the European invasion.

The Indians of the west coast, from southern Alaska to northern California, were primarily fishermen and hunters. In the drier area to the south of them lived the Seed Gatherers, Indians who collected seeds, nuts and berries for food.

The Plains Indians were few in number until the coming of the Europeans, who brought the horse to North America. With the acquisition of horses, Indians moved into the prairies in large numbers to hunt the buffalo herds that roamed there.

In the canyons of the southwest lived one of the oldest cultures of North America, the Basket Makers. These people had developed to a high degree the art of weaving baskets and even fabric from plants, and had learned to make pottery by molding clay inside baskets. They practiced farming and, like Indians throughout America, their staple crop was corn. When threatened by raiding nomads, they built

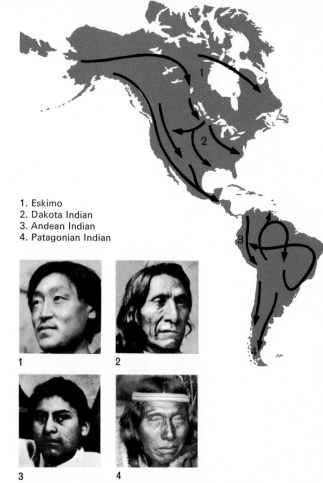

1. Eskimo
2. Dakota Indian
3. Andean Indian
4. Patagonian Indian

Arrows show possible migration routes of Indian ancestors. More than 20,000 years ago a land bridge connected Asia and North America. The first Americans came in this way. Numbers indicate some of the eventual homelands of their descendants.

Great Serpent Mound, Adams County, Ohio. This 1330-foot long snaking earthwork with its foundation of stone, ashes and clay was possibly built by Indians 1500–2000 years ago. The serpent was probably a symbol of religious belief.

Above: warrior from the Osage tribe who originally lived in the lower Ohio valley. Their culture was marked by the alternation of village agriculture and buffalo hunting. During the hunting season Osage Indians lived in movable tepees.
Below: map shows how North American Indians built up different modes of life according to regional natural resources.

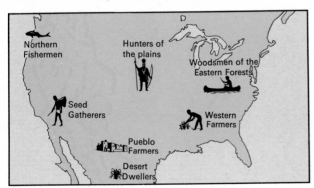

elaborate cliff villages, the ruins of which may still be seen today. When the Spanish explorers arrived, they found the Indians of the southwest living in terraced houses of adobe four or five stories high.

Throughout North America, nomads and villagers alike were governed by chiefs, who in turn were advised by councils of elders. War between tribes tended to be regarded more as an opportunity for displaying bravery than as a means of conquest. Trade was common and barter was the usual method of exchange, although *wampum*, or shell money, was sometimes used by eastern tribes. There were many forms of religion, but most tribes believed in a life after death and thought that a magic power was present in living things. Tribal priests also served as medicine men, and some of the herbal remedies they used are still employed in modern medicines. Almost every tribe had some form of sung poetry and many had musical instruments.

From the Indians, the Europeans learned about tobacco, corn, potatoes, tomatoes, chocolate, vanilla, peppers and many kinds of beans. Snowshoes, canoes and hammocks were Indian inventions, and many American words and place names were taken directly from Indian languages.

Yet when the Europeans arrived, the Indians they found in North America did not possess advanced civilizations. It was farther south, in Middle and South America, that the great Indian civilizations and empires had developed.

143

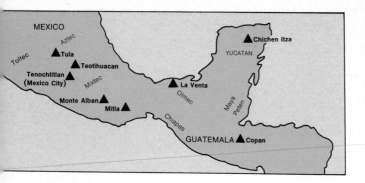

Top: position of Middle America in relation to North and South America.
Left: ancient civilizations in Middle America with location of town sites and tribal groups.

Middle American Civilizations

The first civilization in Middle America known to us is that of the Olmecs, which arose between 1000 and 500 B.C. across a corner of what we now know as Mexico and Guatemala. It flourished especially in the southern coastal area of the Gulf of Mexico.

The Olmecs, whose origins are something of a mystery, built massive temples and other public buildings and had a highly developed and unified art of notable quality and beauty. Jewels and figurines in jade, sculpture and basalt, magnificent white ware and mosaic courtyards bear witness to their artistic sophistication. There are indications also that their achievements included studies for the calendar subsequently perfected by the Mayas, as well as the invention of a form of writing.

But some of the most intriguing of all Olmec relics are their sculptures. Some represent massive heads nine feet long, weighing 15 tons. Others take the form of curiously misshapen dwarfs. What makes all of them specially remarkable is that man managed to carry them without the help of metal tools.

In the last century B.C. there arose in Teotihuacán,

Pages from Maya codex (folding book). Made of bark cloth paper or leather, these codices contain brightly colored picture writing.

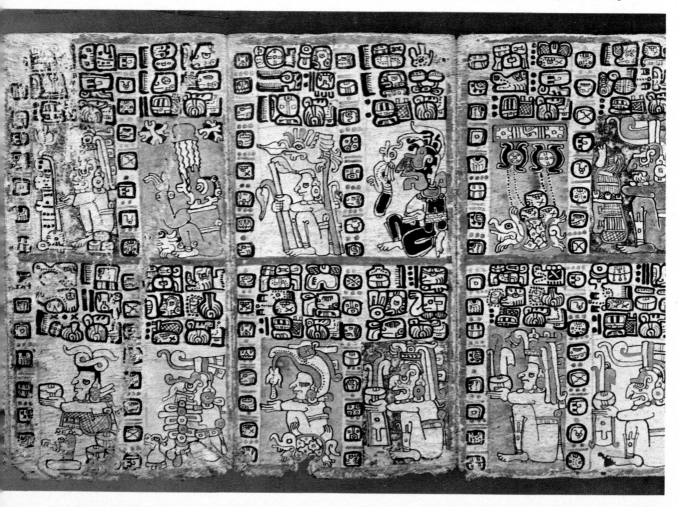

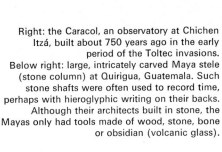

Right: the Caracol, an observatory at Chichen Itzá, built about 750 years ago in the early period of the Toltec invasions. Below right: large, intricately carved Maya stele (stone column) at Quirigua, Guatemala. Such stone shafts were often used to record time, perhaps with hieroglyphic writing on their backs. Although their architects built in stone, the Mayas only had tools made of wood, stone, bone or obsidian (volcanic glass).

a short distance north of what is now the capital of Mexico, a great imperial city of considerable power and cultural influence, though very little is known to us about the Teotihuacános themselves. They were ruled by priest-kings, worshiped a rain god, raised great temples faced with much ornamentation, built impressive avenues and public places, and developed writing and pictorial art.

This ancient center of civilization was unaccountably destroyed in the sixth century A.D. by an unknown invader. But the wide-ranging Teotihuacanos had moved across the Mayan lands over many years and had left their cultural mark there. In the meantime the Olmecs had also moved south and made their cultural contribution.

The flowering of the great but evanescent Maya civilization which followed and absorbed these external influences had its beginnings around A.D. 100. This extraordinary civilization was to reach its full glory between A.D. 300 and 900 and was then utterly lost in a sudden, mysterious collapse.

Of all the early civilizations of the Americas, the Maya was undoubtedly the richest, most brilliant and most urbane. This is the more remarkable in that those who built its finest monuments were lowland peoples of the rain forests and that they chose sites for their magnificent religious and administrative centers in Chiapas and Petén, where every clearing had to be painfully carved from the jungle and constantly protected from its reclamation by the jungle.

The great Maya settlements in what are now Guatemala, Yucatán and bordering states were not cities as we know them, but groupings of small thatched huts in the proximity of great temple pyramids and other buildings, set up for the worship of their gods of earth, rain and wind, and for the housing and training of priest-nobles and acolytes. Even the ball-courts which are a feature of the centers had a religious rather than a recreational purpose. Life was dictated by and revolved about the great religious power houses.

A largely hereditary hierarchy of priest-nobles

ruled each center and there was close and friendly communication between centers, although sharp intertribal wars were not unknown. The Mayas were not quite as gentle a people as may have been thought, although, curiously enough, they appear to have built no defensive works. Eventually mutual economic and cultural concerns led to the forming of a Maya confederation.

The special knowledge and divining powers of the priest-nobles gave the hierarchy a remarkable hold over the mass of the people, whose every activity was ruled by the priestly consultation and propitiation of the appropriate god, a process which included ritual human sacrifice. Prisoners of war, slaves and bastards were the common victims. In lesser rites wild animals were offered up.

The remarkable achievements of the priests and nobles in the field of astronomy and the elaborate rituals and costumes in which they consulted the deities, delivered their findings and conducted other elaborate ceremonies, held the peasants in ready subjection. The ordinary people, wearing only modest breech-clouts, got on with their simple needs and deeds according to the instructions received and they paid their ruler-advisers by generous offerings of time, labor and produce. They grew corn, fruit, cocoa and cotton, kept bees for wax and honey, caught and salted fish, and hunted deer. Life at the bottom was as uncomplicated as it was sophisticated at the top.

Under the instructions of exacting masters and brilliant planners, the Maya people built enormous temples and other structures, often awesome in their siting, height and adornment, but their tools were few and their technical knowledge had great limitations. They never learned how to build a true arch. They never developed the wheel for practical purposes. Everything had to be carried or pulled or pushed without benefit of the wheel and they had no beasts of burden. They had footpaths and local highways and causeways, but no real system of roads.

Yet the Maya achievements in architecture, the arts and astronomy were remarkable by any standards. Indeed, as astronomers they were, in spite of their complete isolation, far in advance of most other peoples in the world. Their endless calculations in a simple system of numbers produced an astonishingly accurate calendar of 18 months of 20 days and one nameless five-day period of special perils.

They were able to do calculations for millions of years backwards in time and, although they were flat-earthers, could predict eclipses of the sun and moon with accuracy. But science largely eluded them and an extravagant mythology ruled their lives.

Although the spoken language has endured to this day and its use roughly marks the extent of the old empire, remains of the written Maya language are few. When these are fully deciphered we shall have a better knowledge of the philosophy as well as the history of these people.

By the end of A.D. 900 the great classic period of the Maya civilization had come to an abrupt, unexplained end. Many theories have been put forward to explain the sudden and almost simultaneous desertion of all the great Maya centers.

The centers were promptly engulfed by the forests when the Mayas mysteriously left them to move into the area of Yucatán. A rebellion of the people against their leaders is one explanation for their flight, and some evidence of deliberate destruction of monuments and images supports this argument. But all we know for certain is that the collapse happened suddenly, so quickly that in some places buildings were left half-finished.

The power vacuum created by the Maya collapse was soon filled. A warlike people arrived from the north, the Toltecs ("Master Builders"), whose capital city, Tula, north of Mexico City, was the

Two 13th or 14th century Zapotec funerary urns. On the left is Cocijo, god of water and flowers. On the right is the figure of a goddess, probably a vegetation spirit. These vases were grouped around the Zapotec dead who were buried in vaults.

Scene from a 14th century wall painting in the Temple of Warriors at Chichen Itzá on the Yucatan Peninsula. Maya temples were small and built on the top of stepped pyramids. Deities included gods of the earth, rain, sun and moon to whom the Mayas made human sacrifices.

administrative center for their considerable empire. Under the leadership of a king who identified himself with Quetzalcoatl, the "Feathered Serpent" of Mexican mythology, the Toltecs made violent assaults on peaceable Maya settlements in coastal Yucatán. The invaders swiftly established themselves and Chichen Itzá, today the famed site of rich archeological remains, became the chief city of the new Toltec-Maya kingdom.

Some of the local Maya chiefs were absorbed into the new ruling order and the old Maya culture itself prevailed to a certain extent alongside the rich new Toltec culture. But Chichen Itzá reflected many features of faraway Tula, which was itself destroyed in civil war, and its character was overwhelmingly Toltec.

The warlike spirit of the arrogant Toltecs found expression in the creation of orders of knighthood, named after jaguars, eagles and coyotes, which were given exaggerated importance, and in the introduction of human sacrifices, following military raids to capture victims, on a scale unknown in Maya territory. But the Toltecs also produced a system of picture symbols which allowed their life and times to be read long after they, too, had vanished suddenly into history, in the 13th century. Their system of picture symbols was picked up by the Mixtecs,

their near kinfolk and a people of notable artistic talent.

Chichen was taken over by the Itzá, a lesser tribe of nomadic warriors, who later founded their own walled city, Mayapan, a poor imitation of the old Toltec center. A Maya rebellion in support of a dissident Mexican family group within its walls led to the destruction and abandonment of Mayapan.

Yucatán itself fell into chaos and an era of darkness began. Only small Mixtec-Maya centers, like the coastal township of Tulum, survived intact in the area as a living remnant of the great civilization of the south on the eve of the Spanish conquest.

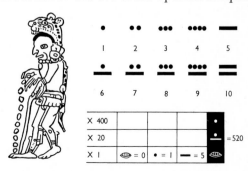

Above: Maya farmer planting corn with a digging stick. Farming and food storage created a need for numeral records. The Maya numeral system is based on 20, a dot equaling one unit and a bar five. Numerals over 20 are written vertically.

147

The Aztec World

During the middle of the 13th century, a nomadic group from the north entered the Valley of Mexico. They were an uncultured people then, poor relations of the Toltecs, whose Nahuatl language they shared. In many places where they tried to settle they were rudely expelled.

This rootless group of Indians went by the name of Aztecs—a word that means "Crane People" and probably refers to their warriors' habit of decorating their hair with crane feathers. Within a short time, it was to become a name that made their enemies tremble throughout Middle America. But at first the Aztecs were held in contempt by the richer and more powerful tribes whose lands they now tried to share.

The dogged Aztecs continued to seek a living space in the area. Their protecting deity, Huitzilopochtli, had said that where they saw an eagle on a cactus grasping a serpent in its talons, they must make their home. They saw it eventually on an island in a lake to which they had come after many setbacks, and here, where no one else had thought fit to live, they made their settlement. They called it Tenochtitlán.

Within a century this seemingly shiftless people had assimilated the old cultural traditions of their neighbors and were on the way to creating an astonishing, if sometimes frightful, civilization. Tenochtitlán became a mighty and magnificent city, the like of which was unknown in contemporaneous Europe. Its palaces and temples, ist streets and canals astonished the Spaniards when, years later, they came upon the city on the lake. It was a splendid, busy, ordered place, pulsating with life. At least a quarter of a million people lived here when the conquistadores arrived.

The wealth and stability of Tenochtitlán had been assured by the military prowess of Itzcoatl, one of its earliest rulers, who made alliances, extended the Aztec territories and exacted high tribute from the subject peoples. His principal adviser, a young relative called Tlacaelel, persuaded him to bring about reforms affecting almost every aspect of Aztec life. Together they rewrote early Aztec history to make it more respectable.

But their major achievement was the complete dedication of Aztec life to religion and warfare through the god Huitzilopochtli, whom they promoted to rank with Quetzalcoatl, the "Plumed Serpent," and Tezcatlipoca, the "Mirror that

Left: 14th century Mixtec knife. The handle, heavily inlaid with turquoise, malachite and shell, is carved in the shape of a crouching eagle knight. The Aztecs conquered the Mixtec people and absorbed their culture.

Right: modern Mexican dressed up as an Aztec warrior at a Mexico City festival. Aztec warriors used to wear ornate plumed headgear like this to inspire awe in the enemy.

Ceremonial feather shield
presented by the Aztec
emperor Montezuma II to Cortés
in 1519. In the center, picked
out in gold, is a coyote.

Smokes," the established deities of the Toltecs. Huitzilopochtli, the "Humming Bird on the Left," became the Sun God and the God of War. He was born and died every day and had to be propitiated by daily gifts of human blood and hearts.

Constant wars were necessary to extend the territories of the Aztecs, to obtain tribute, to punish rebellion, but above all to capture prisoners to offer up to the insatiable Huitzilopochtli and the other gods. The Aztecs were the masters of a world dominated by ill-disposed gods who had to be endlessly placated. Peace was therefore unthinkable.

An elaborate social and administrative system had developed since the crude beginnings in Tenochtitlán. Government was by a council of four, of whom one was supreme, though without absolute powers. The judiciary was independent. Regulations were formulated to govern the army, to direct and protect commercial activities, and to underline the privileges of the higher classes. Education was compulsory for male children.

To give some credibility to their claim to cultural and historical equality with the Toltecs, the Aztecs chose a man of Toltec origin as their first supreme chief. The descendants of this Toltec nobleman were all ennobled to form the *pipiltin*, a special class enjoying better education, better possibilities of advancement and better official appointments.

The Tlatoani, or First Speaker and therefore chief of the Council of Four, was chosen from this class. So was his nominal co-equal, the Cihuacoatl, in charge of local affairs and certain religious matters. The warrior class and its orders of knighthood, the Eagles, Jaguars, and Arrows, enjoyed a special position, as did the priests and the merchants.

The masses worked portions of land assigned to them, on a basis of geographical clans, for communal benefit. They attended their own schools to be trained in warfare and agriculture and those subjects which best served the upper class and the gods. Reading, writing, arithmetic and religious learning were subjects only the *pipiltins* and the other privileged people were allowed to study, and the masses never seem to have disputed their right to them.

149

Priest with stone knife sacrifices victims to Huitzilopochtli, Aztec god of war and of the sun. The Aztecs believed that bloodshed was required constantly, to ensure that the sun would rise each day. Wars were both political and religious; the Aztecs had to take prisoners to sacrifice to their many gods. At the inauguration of the Great Temple of Tenochtitlán 20,000 victims were sacrificed.

There was little in the ordinary processes of Aztec life that was not ordained. Commerce had its own rules and its responsibilities. Markets had to be held at defined intervals. Exchanges of a wide variety of goods, ranging from prized cocoa beans to pottery, rubber to gold, feathers to jade, took place regularly in the appointed markets. The market in Tenochtitlán was particularly impressive. A Spaniard wrote, "Some of our soldiers who had been in many parts of the world, in Constantinople and all over Italy and in Rome said that so large a market place and so full of people and so well regulated and arranged, they had never seen before."

The goods of the far-ranging merchants from Tenochtitlán were carried on foot by porters, because the Aztecs, like the rest of the early Middle Americans, had no beast of burden and had not applied the wheel to the needs of transport. Porters were also used to bring tribute—ranging from such exotic items as fanciful military uniforms to gold, paper and jewels—from the far corners of the empire.

The Aztecs themselves had become first-class craftsmen in many arts, though in most respects they were imitators rather then innovators. They were excellent builders, sculptors, weavers and producers of books whose pictorial symbols later developed into ideographs and a more advanced form of writing. Aztec goldsmiths were among the most skillful craftsmen in the world, and other specialists brought featherwork to a fine art in making priests' clothing out of feathers.

For their warrior heroes they made lethal weapons out of obsidian-edged wooden clubs, spear-throwers, bows and arrows, and a very effective armor of cotton quilting which the Spaniards later adopted for themselves. The masks and head-dresses worn by some of the orders of knighthood were extraordinarily elaborate and no doubt they flattered the wearers as much as they were intended to terrify the enemy.

Far-flung as it was, the Aztec empire was never a cohesive unit. It included people, such as the Cempoaltecas and the Tlaxcaltecas, who resented the Aztec overlordship imposed by threat or by force of arms. The tribute demanded in terms of goods and labor was heavy. These people labored endlessly, forced to deny themselves virtually all comfort in order that the Aztecs might maintain themselves in power and in luxury.

But the Aztecs demanded more than hard work. They actually wanted lives as well. So the subject peoples had to suffer silently the seizure of their young men and maidens as special sacrificial victims in the great temples of Tenochtitlán. The Tlaxcaltecas had to sustain constant armed incursions by Aztec warriors and their trainees, who were bent on capturing prisoners for the same ritual purpose. When the conquistador Cortés marched on Tenochtitlán he found the Cempoaltecas and the Tlaxcaltecas only too ready to become his allies.

Moctecuzoma II, more familiarly known to us in the corrupt form of his name, Montezuma, was Supreme Chief of the Aztecs at the beginning of the 16th century. The Aztec empire was thriving, its frontiers still pushing outwards, especially towards the warm, fertile south. It was a time of great Aztec prosperity, marred only by the announcement of omens of impending disaster.

A whole series of evil signs and portents, starting 10 years before the arrival of the conquistadores,

began to worry Montezuma, his advisers and the Aztec people. There was a comet, a lightning bolt, a fierce storm, a temple on fire, monstrous beings in the streets, the forebodings of a wise woman, fire in the sky, and the netting of a strange fish.

Behind it all was the ever-present threat to Montezuma of the return of Quetzalcoatl, the "Feathered Serpent," who many years before had quit Mexico to go east across the waters, promising to return one day to resume overlordship.

It had been predicted that Quetzalcoatl, a bearded man of fair complexion in his human form, would return in wrath in the irregularly recurring year, "One Reed," corresponding with our 1363, 1467, and 1519. There was no coming of Quetzalcoatl in 1363 or 1467, but 1519 was the year of the coming from across the waters of the Gulf of the bearded, whitefaced Hernán Cortés, Spanish conquistador extraordinary, and Montezuma resigned himself to meet the god come back to challenge him.

Top: Aztec conception of the origin of the universe with a Great God at the center, from a manuscript from southern Mexico. Below: Aztec religious book, used for telling fortunes for the days whose symbols appear in the borders. The book covers a 260-day magic year in 20-day cycles. Made of paper from agave leaves, Aztec books were folded or rolled into scrolls.

Above: Paramonga, a giant Chimú fortress. Built of adobe, this defended the southern boundary of the Chimú kingdom, the largest and most important before the rise of the Incas. Although they had no system of writing the Chimú people developed a highly efficient administrative organisation.

South American Civilizations

Although people had lived in scattered coastal communities in South America for many thousands of years, the first true civilization which emerged was that of the Chavin. They were well established by 1000 B.C. in a valley of the Peruvian Andes and their influence had spread over the northern and central coastal area of Peru.

They appear to have worshiped a feline, perhaps a jaguar, and they built temples for the purpose. They cultivated corn and are thought to have come from the north. The Chavin influenced three other major cultures in the area, the cavern-dwelling Paracas, famous for their embroidery, the warlike Mochicas, who built pyramids of mud bricks, and the Nazcas, who constructed large ceremonial centers and were artistically considerably advanced.

Sometime between A.D. 750 and 900 there existed near Lake Titicaca, high up in what is now Bolivia, the powerful imperial center of another civilization, that of Tiahuanaco. Little is known of its origins and its fate, but remains in the area, including the huge monolithic "Gateway of the Sun," with its representation of a weeping god, suggest that it must be regarded as one of the great lost civili-

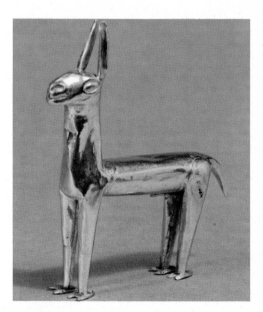

Gold llama, the pack animal of South America, reveals the high level of Inca skill and craftsmanship. Inca metalworkers also made ornaments, implements and arms working in silver, copper and bronze. The Incas constructed public buildings and magnificent city walls using only a few metal tools.

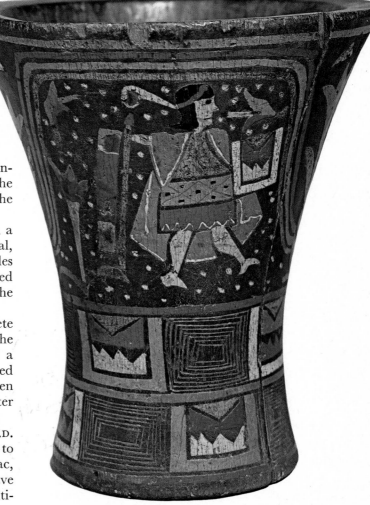

zations of the world. Tiahuanaco's cultural influence spread throughout Peru long before the arrival of the Incas and contributed much to the development of the Nazcas and the Chimú.

The Chimú were another coastal people with a well-developed system of government. Their capital, Chan Chan, covered an area of eight square miles and possessed ordered streets, reservoirs, walled districts, and large temples of adobe dedicated to the worship of the moon.

The Chimú civilization was becoming effete when the Incas arrived on the scene. Like the Aztecs, the Incas were late-comers who waged a relatively quick campaign of conquest, borrowed much from the peoples they vanquished, and then proceeded to retell history for their own greater glory.

It was near the end of the first millennium A.D. that they first made themselves felt. According to one ancient legend, the first Inca, Manco Capac, and his sister-wife, Oyllo, were supposed to have been created by the sun on an island in Lake Titicaca. The sun had sent them to bring civilization to the barbarians of the area and provided them with a golden rod with which to divine the site of their capital city. They found it at Cuzco, the "Navel of the World."

Cuzco became one of the marvels of the Western world, a stone-built city in which some of the massive structures were sheathed in pure gold. It was defended by the fortress of Sacsahuamán, remarkable for its 60-foot-high terraced walls made of close-fitting monolithic stones—a style of building at which the Incas excelled.

Between 1200 and the coming of the Spaniards in 1532, there were 13 Incas or godemperors. All were bent on conquest, seeking power and domination over the peoples of the Andean highland table at first, and then over the coastal plains of the Pacific on one side and the steaming forests of the Amazon on the other.

The most marked progress was made under the ninth Inca, Pachacutec (1438–1471), and his son Tupac. Pachacutec brought important reforms in the social, military and political fields and unleashed a series of crusades against neighboring

peoples. Before Tupac died in 1493 the Inca empire stretched from Argentina to Colombia and from the Pacific to the Amazon. Among the victims of this expansion were the luckless Chimú, who were annihilated.

Their victories put the Incas in control of by far the biggest empire to be built by Amerindian peoples. What was more, they knew how to run it. The Incas were great organizers and administrators. Conquered areas were quickly pacified and absorbed after the imposition of overlords of Inca descent.

In the reign of the 11th Inca, a well-equipped army, said to have numbered 300,000 men, trod the great roads and bridges of the Inca territories in constant pursuit of new triumphs. One of the roads they traveled ran for over 3000 miles, while another climbed to 17,000 feet. The Incas had not invented the wheel, but they did have, in llamas and vicuñas, beasts of burden capable of transporting goods and equipment.

The Incas had not developed writing, but they had a system of numerical recording and communication, based on knotted cords, which could be

153

Bone spatula dating from pre-Inca period (A.D. 400–1000). Inset with turquoise and pyrite nodules, the implement is engraved with the figure of a warrior dressed as a bird.

expanded in range when interpreted by "memory men." By this means Cuzco was kept fully informed of activities everywhere.

Inca society was strictly stratified. At the top was the god-emperor, the Inca. As both man and god he could do no wrong. Any act which was committed against his person or property was sacrilege and severely punished as such.

He had one wife, who was his sister, and many concubines. The succession to the kingship could only come through his sister-wife. Thus divine origin remained unquestioned. The children of the emperor through concubines acquired hereditary nobility automatically. They were given the best posts in the government service. They were permitted as many wives as they chose, but any crimes of which they might be guilty were punished with the outmost severity. The higher the rank, the harder was the penalty.

At the bottom of the social scale were the ordinary people, for the most part peasants. These were largely of Quechua and Aymará stock, the natives of the highlands and coastal plains. They were permitted only one wife. Their basic unit was the ayllú, a sort of clan sharing in common the land, crops and animals apportioned to them by the Inca. The allocation was made on the basis of the number of mouths to be fed. No one was allowed to own land.

These peasants lived in stone-built, thatched houses. They grew potatoes, tomatoes, manioc and cotton and raised guinea pigs and ducks. Llamas and vicuñas served as their beasts of burden, as well as providing them with meat and with the raw wool used in their very skilled weaving.

The self-supporting communities were ruled by an elected leader and a council of elders. Groups of communities were administered by a prefect responsible to the Inca himself.

Produce was subject to tribute after the workers had taken one-third for themselves. Two-thirds went, in equal parts, to the Sun God and the Inca. Additional tribute was levied in the form of work on the construction of great mountain irrigation terraces, temples and other buildings in the cities.

Commerce was a government monopoly and marketing was ordained by edict. Market days and places were often fixed to coincide with the promulgation by word of mouth of new orders from the

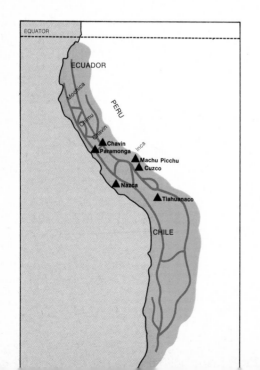

Top: Chimú ear-spool with reversible design. Skilled craftsmen, the Chimú produced excellent gold, silver and copper work. Their culture was based on agriculture, helped by irrigation.
Left: Inca Empire in the 15th century (orange) with the capital Cuzco and the 10,000 miles of tracks used by men and llamas.

Stirrup vases were often molded to represent gods or warriors. Called "stirrup-spouted" because of the two arched tubes ending in a cylindrical spout, these vases are characteristic of both Mochica and Chimú cultures.

Inca masters. Religion, too, was strictly organized.

Clothing was a mark of a man's station. The ordinary man wore a shift and a cape, simply made. The nobility wore clothes of much the same pattern, more richly finished. The Inca himself wore magnificent clothes, often ornamented with rich gold work. They were usually made by the Virgins of the Sun, a sort of order of enclosed nuns. The god-emperor wore each garment only once, after which it was destroyed.

Medicine and surgery were highly developed and many of the medicaments now used throughout the world, quinine among them, were a discovery of the Incas. Astrology and the arts, especially in ceramics, weaving and the working of silver and gold, reached a very high degree of development.

The twelth Inca, Huayna Capac, died before he had named a successor from among his sons. The result was a war between Huascar, the favored son,

and Atahualpa, a younger son. Atahualpa won the struggle after five years and ordered his brother to be killed. He was on his way to Cuzco to become the 13th Inca when news reached him of the arrival of strange white men on the coast.

Strangers to Peru had not been completely unknown in Inca history. As early as the eighth century A.D. Peruvian sailors had traveled 500 miles across the sea to trade with the peoples of the Galapagos Islands. Legends tell of Polynesians from the Marquesas Islands 3,450 sea miles away who visited Peru in the 11th century, and it is conceivable that Chinese junks were carried by wind and current to the shores of South America.

The coming of the Spaniards, however, foreshadowed as in Mexico by portents of ill omen, brought national disaster. When they arrived in 1532, they set about a conquest so ruthless that the entire Inca empire collapsed.

Relics of Inca might and culture. Left: ruins of Macchu Pichu, the 15th century fortress city discovered by an American expedition in 1911. Hidden by the forest, it had lain undisturbed since the departure of its last Inca inhabitants. The city, 8000 feet high on the eastern slopes of the Andes, has temples, compounds and houses overhanging deep abysses—an amazing example of Inca building skill. Top: brightly colored embroidery. Textiles were woven from llama, alpaca or vicuña wool, and cotton. Above: Inca terraces 9000 feet up on the mountainside, built both to prevent soil erosion and extend the amount of farm land.

Time chart (3000 B.C.–A.D.1)

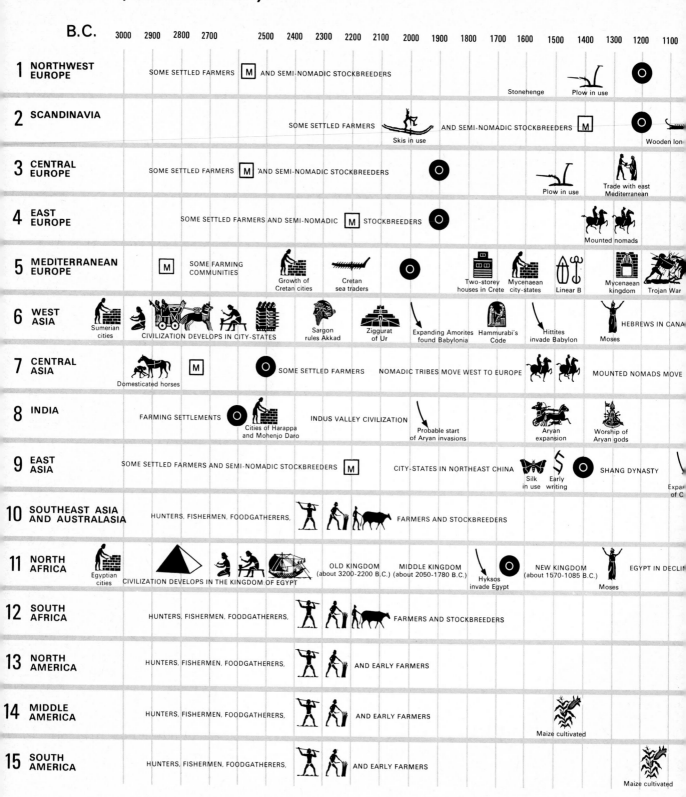

B.C.	3000	2900	2800	2700		2500	2400	2300	2200	2100	2000	1900	1800	1700	1600	1500	1400	1300	1200	1100
1 NORTHWEST EUROPE		SOME SETTLED FARMERS [M] AND SEMI-NOMADIC STOCKBREEDERS														Stonehenge	Plow in use		O	
2 SCANDINAVIA						SOME SETTLED FARMERS		Skis in use		AND SEMI-NOMADIC STOCKBREEDERS						[M]			O	Wooden lon
3 CENTRAL EUROPE		SOME SETTLED FARMERS [M] AND SEMI-NOMADIC STOCKBREEDERS									O						Plow in use	Trade with east Mediterranean		
4 EAST EUROPE			SOME SETTLED FARMERS AND SEMI-NOMADIC [M] STOCKBREEDERS							O							Mounted nomads			
5 MEDITERRANEAN EUROPE		[M] SOME FARMING COMMUNITIES				Growth of Cretan cities		Cretan sea traders			O	Two-storey houses in Crete	Mycenaean city-states		Linear B		Mycenaean kingdom		Trojan War	
6 WEST ASIA	Sumerian cities	CIVILIZATION DEVELOPS IN CITY-STATES				Sargon rules Akkad		Ziggurat of Ur		Expanding Amorites found Babylonia	Hammurabi's Code		Hittites invade Babylon		Moses		HEBREWS IN CANA			
7 CENTRAL ASIA	Domesticated horses		[M]		SOME SETTLED FARMERS				NOMADIC TRIBES MOVE WEST TO EUROPE							MOUNTED NOMADS MOVE				
8 INDIA		FARMING SETTLEMENTS		Cities of Harappa and Mohenjo Daro		INDUS VALLEY CIVILIZATION					Probable start of Aryan invasions		Aryan expansion		Worship of Aryan gods					
9 EAST ASIA		SOME SETTLED FARMERS AND SEMI-NOMADIC STOCKBREEDERS [M]					CITY-STATES IN NORTHEAST CHINA			Silk in use	Early writing	O	SHANG DYNASTY						Expan of C	
10 SOUTHEAST ASIA AND AUSTRALASIA	HUNTERS, FISHERMEN, FOODGATHERERS,					FARMERS AND STOCKBREEDERS														
11 NORTH AFRICA	Egyptian cities	CIVILIZATION DEVELOPS IN THE KINGDOM OF EGYPT				OLD KINGDOM (about 3200-2200 B.C.)		MIDDLE KINGDOM (about 2050-1780 B.C.)			Hyksos invade Egypt	O	NEW KINGDOM (about 1570-1085 B.C.)				Moses	EGYPT IN DECLI		
12 SOUTH AFRICA	HUNTERS, FISHERMEN, FOODGATHERERS,					FARMERS AND STOCKBREEDERS														
13 NORTH AMERICA	HUNTERS, FISHERMEN, FOODGATHERERS,					AND EARLY FARMERS														
14 MIDDLE AMERICA	HUNTERS, FISHERMEN, FOODGATHERERS,					AND EARLY FARMERS										Maize cultivated				
15 SOUTH AMERICA	HUNTERS, FISHERMEN, FOODGATHERERS,					AND EARLY FARMERS													Maize cultivated	

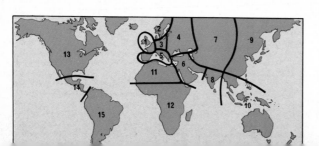

World History Time Chart

This chart gives a comparative view of man's development in many fields and many cultures. It is divided into 15 regions, each unit having, broadly speaking, a single cultural tradition. The numbers on the chart correspond to the numbered regions on the accompanying map.

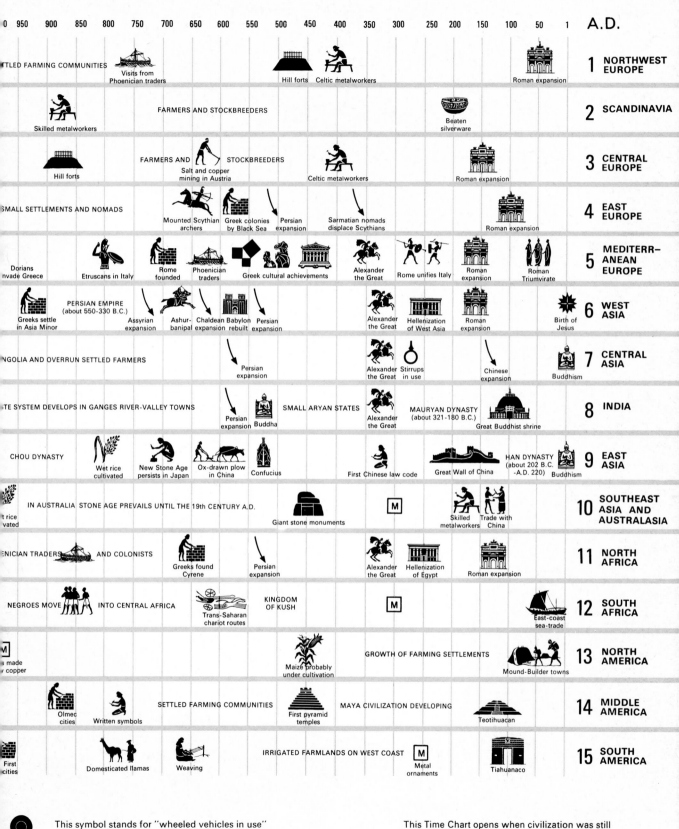

Timeline scale (B.C. to A.D.): 950 900 850 800 750 700 650 600 550 500 450 400 350 300 250 200 150 100 50 1 A.D.

1 NORTHWEST EUROPE — SETTLED FARMING COMMUNITIES · Visits from Phoenician traders · Hill forts · Celtic metalworkers · Roman expansion

2 SCANDINAVIA — Skilled metalworkers · FARMERS AND STOCKBREEDERS · Beaten silverware

3 CENTRAL EUROPE — Hill forts · FARMERS AND STOCKBREEDERS · Salt and copper mining in Austria · Celtic metalworkers · Roman expansion

4 EAST EUROPE — SMALL SETTLEMENTS AND NOMADS · Mounted Scythian archers · Greek colonies by Black Sea · Persian expansion · Sarmatian nomads displace Scythians · Roman expansion

5 MEDITERRANEAN EUROPE — Dorians invade Greece · Etruscans in Italy · Rome founded · Phoenician traders · Greek cultural achievements · Alexander the Great · Rome unifies Italy · Roman expansion · Roman Triumvirate

6 WEST ASIA — Greeks settle in Asia Minor · PERSIAN EMPIRE (about 550-330 B.C.) · Assyrian expansion · Ashurbanipal · Chaldean Babylon rebuilt · Persian expansion · Alexander the Great · Hellenization of West Asia · Roman expansion · Birth of Jesus

7 CENTRAL ASIA — ...NGOLIA AND OVERRUN SETTLED FARMERS · Persian expansion · Alexander the Great · Stirrups in use · Chinese expansion · Buddhism

8 INDIA — ...TE SYSTEM DEVELOPS IN GANGES RIVER-VALLEY TOWNS · Persian expansion · Buddha · SMALL ARYAN STATES · Alexander the Great · MAURYAN DYNASTY (about 321-180 B.C.) · Great Buddhist shrine

9 EAST ASIA — CHOU DYNASTY · Wet rice cultivated · New Stone Age persists in Japan · Ox-drawn plow in China · Confucius · First Chinese law code · Great Wall of China · HAN DYNASTY (about 202 B.C.-A.D. 220) · Buddhism

10 SOUTHEAST ASIA AND AUSTRALASIA — ...t rice ...vated · IN AUSTRALIA STONE AGE PREVAILS UNTIL THE 19th CENTURY A.D. · Giant stone monuments · M · Skilled metalworkers · Trade with China

11 NORTH AFRICA — ...ENICIAN TRADERS AND COLONISTS · Greeks found Cyrene · Persian expansion · Alexander the Great · Hellenization of Egypt · Roman expansion

12 SOUTH AFRICA — NEGROES MOVE INTO CENTRAL AFRICA · Trans-Saharan chariot routes · KINGDOM OF KUSH · M · East-coast sea-trade

13 NORTH AMERICA — ...s made ...y copper · Maize probably under cultivation · GROWTH OF FARMING SETTLEMENTS · Mound-Builder towns

14 MIDDLE AMERICA — Olmec cities · Written symbols · SETTLED FARMING COMMUNITIES · First pyramid temples · MAYA CIVILIZATION DEVELOPING · Teotihuacan

15 SOUTH AMERICA — First cities · Domesticated llamas · Weaving · IRRIGATED FARMLANDS ON WEST COAST · M Metal ornaments · Tiahuanaco

This symbol stands for "wheeled vehicles in use" —a key landmark in man's cultural development.

M Metalworking—one of the basic skills of civilization and a yardstick for measuring its progress.

This Time Chart opens when civilization was still young in Sumer and Egypt, though both were using metals and Sumerians had invented wheeled vehicles. Between 1000 B.C.-A.D. 1 expanded time units cope with the increasingly complex pattern of events, including the emergence of empires.